NEGOTIATING CONSENT
IN PSYCHOTHERAPY

QUALITATIVE STUDIES IN PSYCHOLOGY

This series showcases the power and possibility of qualitative work in psychology. Books feature detailed and vivid accounts of qualitative psychology research using a variety of methods, including participant observation and field work, discursive and textual analyses, and critical cultural history. They probe vital issues of theory, implementation, representation, and ethics that qualitative workers confront. The series mission is to enlarge and refine the repertoire of qualitative approaches to psychology.

GENERAL EDITORS

Michelle Fine and Jeanne Marecek

Everyday Courage:
The Lives and Stories of Urban Teenagers
by Niobe Way

Negotiating Consent in Psychotherapy
by Patrick O'Neill

NEGOTIATING CONSENT
IN PSYCHOTHERAPY

PATRICK O'NEILL

New York University Press
New York and London

NEW YORK UNIVERSITY PRESS
New York and London

Library of Congress Cataloging-in-Publication Data
O'Neill, Patrick, 1942–
Negotiating consent in psychotherapy / Patrick O'Neill.
p.   cm.   —   (Qualitative studies in psychology)
Includes bibliographical references (p.   ) and index.
ISBN 0-8147-6194-1 (cloth : acid-free paper)
ISBN 0-8147-6195-X (paper : acid-free paper)
1. Psychotherapist and patient. 2. Therapeutic alliance.
3. Informed consent (Medical law)   I. Title. II. Series.
RC480.8 .O54 1998
616.89'14—ddc21   98-25349
                         CIP

New York University Press books are printed on acid-free paper,
and their binding materials are chosen for strength and durability.

Manufactured in the United States of America

10   9   8   7   6   5   4   3   2   1

■ ■ ■ ■ ■
For J.J.

Contents

■ ■ ■   ■

Acknowledgments

The interviews presented in this book were carried out by Stefani Hurley and Elaine Campbell, whose skill and sensitivity ensured that I had a wealth of material to work with. Stephen Shaw coded and abstracted interview material during what we will always remember as the long, hot summer of '97. Angela MacKay assisted Stephen in a review of relevant literature. Wendy Nickerson and Janice Davidson transcribed audiotapes.

Janice Best worked closely with me on the notion of a therapy narrative constructed by therapist and client. She gave me many suggestions regarding the conceptual framework of this book, including pointing out the relevance to this project of the ideas of Frank Kermode, Umberto Eco, and Mikhail Bakhtin.

The interviews for this study were conducted and analyzed with the help of the Social Sciences and Humanities Research Council of Canada, whose support included three generous research grants, and of the Canadian Association of University Teachers, which bought research time for me while I was on the Executive Committee of that body.

■ ■ ■ ■ ■ ■ ■ ■ ■

Introduction

Therapy as Narrative Structure

When client meets therapist, they begin the construction of a therapy narrative, with a beginning, a middle, and an end. The beginning is a conception of where the problem came from. The middle is an understanding of what will happen in therapy. The end is an idea about what the result will be, how the client will function when therapy has run its course.

The therapy narrative is a product of separate narratives that client and therapist bring to the enterprise. Each is an expert in a different domain. Clients are experts on their own lives and on the sorts of persons they want to be when therapy is finished. Therapists are experts on the therapeutic process, especially on their preferred approach. They also have clinical knowledge gained from their work with clients with similar problems. They can estimate, on the basis of that experience, the likelihood of various outcomes.

Clients and therapists have flaws in their expertise, of course. Clients may have repressed traumatic memories that turn out to be significant life events of which they were unaware. Their notions of a good outcome may change in the course of treatment. Therapists may apply the model on which their approach is based even though it does not fit the circumstances of a particular client (for instance, they may search for memories of events that never happened). They may apply knowledge gained from clients of a certain sort to a client whose case is different in some important way. Despite these flaws, it remains the case that client and therapist have different realms in which they can be considered, generally speaking, to have special knowledge that the other does not have.

When they begin to work together, therapists and clients also have notions about the middle of the story, the space where therapy occurs. Therapists have more precise knowledge about therapy, since they have done it before, and often with clients who have similar problems. But clients, too, come to treatment with expectations. These may be based on previous therapy experiences or on what they have been told by family and friends, or through exposure to popular media. However they get their information, they do not come into the process without expectations.

Since clients and therapists start with their own narratives, at some point they have to construct a joint narrative that includes an agreed beginning, middle, and end: This is how the problem arose in *this* case; this is what *we* will do in therapy; this would be a satisfactory outcome. Such construction requires negotiation from the first minutes of the first session to the end of the process. Negotiation needs to be ongoing, because ideas about causes, process, and outcome are fluid and will change over the course of therapy.

All situations constrain the narratives that are possible within them. In therapy, there is a general narrative that is constrained by certain requirements of the therapy situation. The client must have a problem for which a cause will be sought, a treatment will be constructed, and a plausible positive result can be imagined. The therapist must take on a helping role, be prepared to explore the client's ideas about the problem, and have some background knowledge that is potentially relevant. These are minimum criteria for the *therapy narrative*.

An example of a violation of the therapy narrative is the client who comes claiming to have no problem. Faced with such a client, therapists see their first task as getting agreement that there *is* a problem so that some variation on the therapy narrative can unfold. Similarly, the therapy narrative requires that a therapist be engaged in trying to understand and help a client. It is not consistent with the therapy narrative, for example, that the client be nurturing helper for the therapist (it may happen, but it is not therapy).

Within the therapy narrative, there are a wide variety of stories that can be constructed by client and therapist. But these are constrained by the knowledge and assumptions of the partners in the therapeutic venture. The information clients have about their own lives fits some constructions but not others. If a client has no memory of childhood sexual abuse and believes it never happened, a narrative in which her problem is the result of abuse will not work. There are similar constraints on the stories therapists can construct. If a therapist believes, by training and experience, that anorexic patients are always afraid of mature sexual relationships, a narrative in which the client is starving to make herself attractive (and sexually active) will not work.

The therapist or the client may have the facts wrong, of course. The client may have repressed the memory of early abuse. The therapist's beliefs about anorexic patients may be true of only some cases. But as long as client and therapist are locked into sets of incompatible facts, they will find it difficult to coordinate their narratives to accommodate what each believes to be the facts of the case. A difference in viewpoints may be required to create the productive tension that makes change possible. But their stories must have some overlap if therapist and client are to forge a therapeutic alliance. The need to coordinate narratives may require considerable negotiation.

This book is about that process of negotiation, and in particular about negotiation of consent. I focus on consent for two reasons: first, it is important in itself as an ethical issue in treatment; second, there are professional and legal pressures on therapists to obtain free and informed consent, and we ought to see negotiation here if we are to see it anywhere. Those pressures are increasing; for example, there are legal standards that require therapists not only to say what their own therapy entails but also to indicate the alternatives available. Because these alternatives are often based on different conceptions of the problem, true informed consent would seem to require a discussion of these conceptions with the client. Since many therapists believe that material of this sort is best left for later sessions after certain groundwork has been done, negotiation of consent becomes a process that could (perhaps should) continue over the course of therapy.

Influences

There are many strands of thought that come together in the theory of therapy I have just outlined. I will use and elaborate this conceptual framework, and relate it to data, at various points in the book. For the moment, I want to acknowledge a few important progenitors.

Frank Kermode (1967) suggested that we organize our experience in narrative form. A narrative is "a bundling together of the present, memory of the past, and expectation of the future in a common organization" (p. 46). We create these narratives to establish beginnings and endings that render the present coherent. Thus, present becomes charged with past and future. In Kermode's view, we have a permanent need to "live by the pattern rather than the fact" (p. 11), but we also feel a need to respect things as they are. This conflict between the pattern and the facts produces a recurring need for adjustments to our unfolding life stories. Without adjustments that respect reality, we would lose what control we have over what happens to us. As Kermode puts it, since we cannot break free of events, we must make sense of them.

Umberto Eco (1984) goes into more detail on the way in which we interpret events to create narratives. Our world is experienced step by step, and at each step we are led to wonder what will happen at the next step. We are continually framing hypotheses. He calls this process "taking inferential walks" (p. 31). These mental walks move us beyond the immediate situation and help us interpret it with the help of our past experience, including assumptions made available by our culture. But experience, both personal and cultural, is rich enough to support a variety of interpretations of what is presently going on and what will happen next. Thus, an inferential walk opens many narrative structures, some more plausible than others. Each of these narratives Eco calls "a possible world" (p. 219), defined as a possible course of events. The next step we take depends on the possible world that seems most plausible, given the inferences we have made about what is happening now.

Kenneth Gergen and Mary Gergen have both advanced social constructionist and relational approaches to psychotherapy. Ken Gergen, referring to the coconstruction of meaning in therapy (1994, 1997) talks about the collaborative discourse between therapist and client, a potentially transformative dialogue in which new understandings are negotiated together. This negotiation is at the heart of the therapist-client relationship, in which the meaning of experience is transformed through "a fusion of the horizons of the participants" (Gergen and Kaye, 1992, p. 182). At its best, psychotherapy is a receptive mode of inquiry open to different ways of interpreting experience and ready to explore multiple perspectives—what Eco calls possible worlds—and to endorse their coexistence. Mary Gergen (1994) proposes that therapist and client be seen as forming a relational unit that produces selves within and through interaction: "Rather than the therapist as expert, the power relationships become equalized" (p. 20). Such equality can be achieved only if there is reasonably full negotiation between therapist and client about what is happening, what will happen, and, in the case of alternatives, what could happen.

Putting some of these influences together: Kermode points to our need to create narratives to understand our lives; Eco says our experience is always sufficiently complex to permit a variety of interpretations about the past and (especially) about the future; the Gergens emphasize the coconstructed and relational nature of psychotherapy.

The Study

The data for this qualitative study were gathered in ninety-two interviews with therapists and clients over a five-year period. The therapists, who had a variety of professional backgrounds, all considered themselves specialists in one or more of three areas: treating eating disorders, working with survivors of childhood sexual abuse, or treating sex offenders. The clients all fell into at least one of those categories.

The guiding questions of the study were: What do therapists believe should be part of consent, and why? When do they obtain such consent, and how do they decide when it should be renegotiated? How do clients experience the process?

What This Book Is Not

This is not intended to be a how-to-do-it manual about consent. It is, rather, an exploration of how therapists cope with the demands to negotiate consent with their clients and how clients perceive this process.

At times, I will mark particular negotiations described by therapists as exemplifying the ideas embodied in the conception of therapy I have proposed. Nevertheless, this book is not an exposé of bad practice. There are many varieties of the right way to do things, and naming one practice as exemplary does not mean that other narratives represent inadequacies. This generally nonjudgmental approach reflects my view that the process of negotiation, including negotiation of informed consent, is a complex and difficult business. My purpose is to explore how those complexities, even contradictions, are dealt with in psychotherapy.

The interviews are all reflections of the views of therapists and clients at the time we spoke with them. They often talk about different points in therapy (for instance, what happens at the start, how therapy ends, and so on). Nevertheless the nature of the present study rules out a study of ongoing process. For those interested in that topic, I recommend the excellent work on psychotherapy process by McMullen and Conway (1994), Angus and Hardtke (1994), and Toukmanian and Rennie (1992).

Finally, this is not a book about therapy with children. Issues are different when the client is a child and consent must be sought from parents or guardians. I have chosen to focus on adult clients, where there is a reasonable expectation that therapist and client will negotiate the business of therapy together. The only exception concerns some examples of adolescents with eating disorders who may be on the cusp of the age of consent. In these cases, therapists usually assume that they need to obtain consent from the client, not just from parents.

A Note on Terms

This study comprises almost a hundred interviews involving both therapists and clients. To help keep them straight: When interview material is presented, each segment is followed by a code such as (T^{23}), which indicates that the speaker was a therapist and it was interview number twenty-three. Similarly, (C^{18}) at the end of a segment indicates both a client and the eighteenth interview.

An author must decide when to use "I" and when to use "we." In this book I use the singular, as now, when talking about what I, as author, am doing (or thinking or claiming). I use the plural when including the reader

("As we will see in the next chapter . . .") or when including my research team ("Our interviews suggested . . .").

The label "survivor" is now preferred over "victim" for persons who are coping with traumatic events such as child abuse or spouse battering. The former term is thought to be empowering. (Nevertheless, there has also been criticism of the use of "survivor"; see Anderson and Gold, 1994). In this book I use the term "survivor" most of the time. But I use "victim" when the focus is on the fact of being victimized, as in: "Some offenders claim they were victims."

Outline of the Book

Chapter 1 is a discussion of the history of consent in the health professions from the time of Hippocrates to the Nuremberg Code. I focus on recent legal and ethical developments that have put pressure on therapists to provide information to clients not only about their own proposed treatment but also about alternative treatments and alternative conceptions of the problem.

Chapter 2 describes the interviews collected for this book, and the interview process itself. I discuss interviewing as a method in qualitative research and locate my approach in that domain.

Chapter 3 turns from how questions are asked to how the answers are understood. The focus is on qualitative analysis; I present my approach and contrast it with other approaches. The main task of analysis, as I see it, is to help participants to tell their stories. The purpose is to explore the richness of the phenomena by finding common threads and different strands across and among accounts of formally similar experiences.

Chapters 4, 5, and 6 present accounts from therapists and clients about negotiation in therapy. Each chapter focuses on a different problem area: people with eating disorders, survivors of sexual abuse, and sex offenders.

Chapter 4 is concerned with negotiation of consent in therapy for eating disorders such as anorexia and bulimia. Clients are often adolescents; thus, there may be pressure to include parents in the consent process. Therapists differ about whether the family is a cause of the problem, a source of help in dealing with it, or both. There are many different views about the value of family involvement in treatment and many conceptions of eating disorders and the best treatment for them. This leads to a rich field of possibilities that can be explored with the client. We will see a variety of ways in which therapists use this opportunity for negotiation, as seen by therapists and by clients. In some cases we have data from therapists about what they do and from clients of those same therapists about what they experienced.

Chapter 5 concerns survivors of childhood sexual abuse. A major theme in this area is the loss of control and destruction of trust that result from early victimization. There is general agreement (always with interesting exceptions) that negotiation of consent is extremely important in this domain because of the need to empower clients and to establish trust in an authority figure. Within the context of this theme of trust and control, there are fewer specific treatments than for eating disorders. Our interviews touch on other negotiation issues that arise in this area, such as whether the adult client should be encouraged to report childhood sexual abuse. What are the costs and benefits of moving from the therapeutic context to the legal system? Finally, there is conflict between those who emphasize the need to recover repressed memories of abuse and those who fear the creation of false memories. This controversy is mirrored in our data, which includes therapists (and clients) on both sides of the issue and therapists who accept aspects of both sides and try to find a reasonable compromise in their daily work.

Chapter 6 is devoted to problems of negotiation in treatment of sex offenders. Therapy usually occurs in the framework of the legal system, which puts severe constraints on the freedom to consent. Most therapists who work with this population consider such constraints to be essential because they perceive their clients to be extremely manipulative. Our participants include, in addition to a variety of therapists, two clients in treatment for abusing children.

The major debate in this field is between those who attempt to induce empathy in offenders and those who use arousal training to decrease recidivism. Our participants have something to say on that issue, as well as on such treatment options as having women as therapists for male abusers, and the current vogue for one-size-fits-all group treatment programs.

There is overlap between conditions presented in these three data-filled chapters. For example, there are many people who come into therapy because of eating disorders who have also been sexually abused (chapters 4 and 5). The issue of which problem to address first is a serious one for clients and therapists. Many sex offenders claim that they themselves were sexually abused (chapters 5 and 6). Therapists differ on the extent to which they take such reports to be problems for treatment or manipulative excuses for antisocial behavior. Two therapists presented in chapters 5 and 6 deal with young men and adolescents who are both abusers and abused at the same time, raising a host of questions about the therapist's contradictory obligations to respect confidentiality or to protect the public.

Chapter 7 draws together the various strands from our interview material to see what patterns emerge. What can be said about negotiation in therapy, at least in these three treatment domains and at least with regard to consent, on the basis of our encounters with therapists and clients? The notion that therapy involves coconstruction is elaborated, and findings of the present investigation are put into that larger context.

1

■ ■   ■   ■   ■   ■   ■   ■   ■

Informed Consent as a Challenge
for Psychotherapists

HIPPOCRATES and his followers had no interest in the sort of informed consent we now consider essential in health care. The father of medical ethics, who lived and worked around 400 B.C., is remembered for his oath, which emphasized the physician's obligation to do no harm and to maintain confidentiality. But there is nothing in the writing of Hippocrates and his followers to indicate that patients should have meaningful input into treatment decisions. On the contrary, in *Decorum,* attributed to Hippocrates, apprentice physicians are given this advice about bedside manner:

> Perform all this calmly and adroitly, concealing most things from the patient while you are attending to him. Turn his attention away from what is being done to him. Sometimes reprove [him] sharply and emphatically, and sometimes comfort with solicitude and attention, revealing nothing of the patient's future or present. (Hippocrates, 1923).

The *Precepts* give more advice about the lengths to which the healer should go in concealing information from patients:

> And yet some patients ask for what is out of the way and doubtful, through prejudice, deserving indeed to be disregarded, but not to be punished.

Wherefore you must readily oppose them, as they are embarked upon a stormy sea of change. (Hippocrates, 1923)

This strong view that the doctor knows best and that the patient's role is to be compliant and to follow medical advice continued to be a touchstone of the healing arts for more than two millennia. Only in the second half of the twentieth century was there a shift from reliance on the doctor's judgment to a belief in the right of the patient or client to self-determination.

On this older view, not only were patients' views of treatment irrelevant, but it was thought best to keep them in the dark about their condition. Although there were occasional dissenters, the prevailing view among healers was that too much information would merely confuse patients; where the malady was serious, knowledge might actually be harmful.

The idea that patients may be or ought to be deceived for their own good became enshrined in *therapeutic privilege*, a doctrine that holds that the healer may withhold information that he or she believes would be harmful to the patient. This doctrine, long an implicit fact of practice, was formally enunciated in Thomas Percival's influential *Medical Ethics* (Percival, 1849).

Although this was the orthodox position, there were always some dissenters. Samuel Johnson, in 1784, thundered against doctors who lied to their patients for fear of alarming them. He said that doctors had no business worrying about the consequences of truthfulness. "You are to tell the truth. Besides, you are not sure what effect your telling him that he is in danger may have. It may bring his distemper to a crisis, and that may cure him" (Boswell's *Life of Johnson*, June 13, 1784, cited in Percival, 1849). Percival quoted Johnson's view merely to attack it in his *Medical Ethics*.

Percival claimed if knowledge would harm patients, it would be "a gross and unfeeling wrong" to tell them the truth. He maintained that a patient's right to the truth is "suspended, even annihilated" by the patient's stronger right to be kept from harm. He went beyond arguing that one may lie to patients and claimed that to deceive a dejected or sick patient, as long as the objective is to give hope, is not a lie.

Like Samuel Johnson, Worthington Hooker was a critic of the orthodox position. In *Physician and Patient* (1849), he raised a number of arguments against deceiving patients: Doctors are often wrong in thinking that the truth will hurt the patient; the patient usually finds out the truth anyway; discovery of the deception by the patient has a worse effect than the truth would have had; the deceived patient, upon learning the truth, loses confidence in the doctor; other people, seeing that doctors lie to their patients, lose confidence in the profession; once deception is allowed in some cases, it is hard to place limits on it. Hooker disagreed with Percival and others who said that deception is acceptable in urgent cases. He pointed out that deception succeeds only if patients believe that doctors tell them the truth. If they realize that patients are deceived in *some* cases, they will not trust what they say in *any* cases. Thus, lying becomes self-defeating.

Despite arguments of this sort, the doctrine of therapeutic privilege remained an important principle of medical practice. Joseph Collins, writing in the 1920s, defended lying to patients. He argued that patients say "tell me the truth" but usually do not mean it. Even if they do, some would be injured by the truth. He commented, "The longer I practice medicine the more convinced I am that every physician should cultivate lying as a fine art" (Collins, 1927, p. 321).

Beyond the debate about outright deception, physicians tended to think that the patient would not have much to offer about what treatment should be administered. In fact, patients were discouraged from informing themselves so that they might have something to say. This is evident in the first Code of Ethics of the American Medical Association, published in 1847. Although such codes are designed to inform and guide professionals, this code was as much concerned about obligations of patients to their physicians as those that doctors have to their patients:

> The obedience of the patient to the prescriptions of his physician should be prompt and implicit. He should never permit his own crude opinions as to their fitness to influence his attention to them. . . . A patient should never send for a consulting physician without the express consent of his own medical attendant. He should never converse [with other physicians] on the subject of his disease, as an observation may be made . . . which may destroy his confidence in the course he is pursuing. (American Medical Association, 1847)

The legal system has been somewhat more demanding of doctors with regard to consent. Silverman reports that, in 1767, a British judge said, "A patient should be told what is about to be done to him, that he may take courage and put himself in such a situation as to enable him to undergo the operation." Once the patient had been told, the judge said, he could "vote with his feet." Voluntary submission was taken as proof of consent (Silverman, 1989, p. 6).

A landmark ruling came at the beginning of the twentieth century, when Judge Benjamin Cordozo, writing in a New York case, said, "Every human being of adult years and sound mind has a right to determine what shall be done with his own body." As Pope and Vasquez (1991) point out, Judge Cordozo made it clear that it was the patient rather than the doctor who had the right to decide about a specific treatment approach. But, they add, "The implications of this principle lay dormant for decades" (p. 76).

The courts, as well as health professionals, often take a paternalistic attitude toward persons thought to be in need of treatment. Judge Cordozo's principle has sometimes been upheld, but in other cases it has been ignored. Courts have ruled that patients of sound mind can be compelled to have treatment if they have dependent children or if the judge takes the view that treatment is what they really want as opposed to what they say they want (Appelbaum, Lidz, and Meisel, 1987).

The Influence of Nuremberg

The major change in thinking that emphasized free and informed consent occurred after World War II. The Nuremberg trials were held to judge and expose the abuses of human rights in Nazi Germany. Among other abuses, the trials dealt with the notorious medical experiments in concentration camps, some of which were done in the context of "treatment."

Out of the trials came the *Nuremberg Code on Medical Intervention and Experimentation* (1964/1945). This Code specified that voluntary consent of the human subject is absolutely essential in medical research and treatment. The person involved should be so situated as to able to exercise free power of choice and should have sufficient knowledge and comprehension of the treatment or research to permit an understanding and enlightened decision (Nuremberg Code 1964/1945).

The two main ways of protecting the public from the healer are oversight and consent. Throughout most of the history of healing, the emphasis was on oversight: monitoring of professional activity by professional associations, regulatory bodies, or the courts. The Nuremberg Declaration gave a new, privileged position to consent, putting control into the hands of the client.

The ideas found in the Nuremberg Code were echoed in the World Medical Association's *Helsinki Declaration*, which was drafted in 1964 and later revised several times. (The latest incarnation is the *Helsinki-Tokyo Declaration*, usually called "Helsinki II.") This declaration is directed at research and combined research-treatment situations. Potential subjects, says the Declaration, must be adequately informed of the aims, methods, anticipated benefits, and potential hazards of the study. They must be told that they are free not to participate and free to withdraw at any time (World Medical Association, 1975).

The importance of free and informed consent has been enshrined in a wide variety of professional codes of ethics, such as those of the American Psychiatric Association (1989) and the American Psychological Association (1990). The most recent revision of the code of the American Psychological Association spells out these requirements for consent:

> 4.02(a) psychologists obtain appropriate informed consent to therapy or related procedures, using language that is reasonably understandable to participants. The content of informed consent will vary depending on the circumstances; however informed consent generally implies that the person . . . has been informed of significant information concerning the procedure . . . has freely and without undue influence expressed consent. (American Psychological Association, 1990)

Other codes contain the same basic material with various flourishes and additions. The National Association of Social Workers (1989) adds that consent includes agreement regarding the goals of treatment. The Canadian Psychological Association (1991) gives rationales drawn from moral philosophy for each of its main principles. Its first principle, based on the writings of Immanuel Kant, is "respect for the dignity of persons," which includes the right to self-determination and thus to informed consent.

Health providers have been encouraged to give importance to informed consent by external bodies such as granting agencies and the courts.

The Changing Legal Situation

Before 1950 the duty to inform the client and to get the client's consent was primarily what is called in law a *negative duty*. That is, false information was prohibited; one could not say that a treatment was something that it was not or that it would have an outcome that the therapist knew to be unlikely or impossible. But no specific information, even about possible risks, had to be provided.

A group of cases in the 1950s changed the duty from a negative to a positive one. In a North Carolina case, *Hunt v. Bradshaw* (1955), the judge asserted that it was no longer sufficient merely not to deceive; now, it was necessary to provide information about the condition and the treatment—especially the risks involved.

The North Carolina case provided a precedent for a number of others that followed. One of these, *Salgo v. Stanford University* (1957), is noteworthy because it gave us the phrase "informed consent." Aside from coining this phrase, though, the Salgo case merely muddled matters. The court decreed that a doctor may withhold alarming information from a patient, "consistent, of course, with the full disclosure of the facts necessary to an informed consent" (cited in Appelbaum, Lidz, and Meisel, 1987, p. 39). Here, the court was trying to uphold both therapeutic privilege (the right to withhold information) and the right of the patient to know all the facts. Other courts became quite confused when trying to use the *Salgo* decision as a precedent. In a New York case the following year, a physician was found liable for mental anguish caused by information he disclosed to the patient about her condition and its treatment (Appelbaum, Lidz, and Meisel, 1987).

Some 1960 cases finally tipped the balance in favor of the client's right to know. One of these was *Mitchell v. Robinson*, which involved a woman who received insulin shock and electroconvulsive therapy (ECT) as a treatment for schizophrenia; the treatment fractured several vertebrae. The judge established the notion of an *affirmative* duty, a requirement to inform the patient about the possible hazards of treatment.

The courts were now telling practitioners that they had to provide "sufficient" information, rather than try to spare the patient's feelings. But what should be the standard for how much information is sufficient? There are two ground-breaking cases on this point; one established the "reasonable doctor" standard in 1960, and the second replaced it with the "reasonable patient" standard a dozen years later. These are very different standards, and they have ethical and legal consequences for health practitioners.

The "reasonable doctor" standard had been implicitly relied on by the courts for some time before it was clearly articulated in *Natanson v. Kline* (1960):

> The duty to disclose is limited to those procedures which a reasonable practitioner would make under the same or similar circumstances . . . the physician's choice of plausible courses should not be called into question if . . . the physician was motivated by the patient's best therapeutic interests and he proceeded as competent medical men would have done in a similar situation. (Cited in Pope and Vasquez, 1991, p. 76)

Using this standard, a professional was expected to provide the sort of information that other members of the profession typically gave to their clients in similar situations. Pope and Vasquez (1991) refer to this as the *community standard* rule: "Informed consent procedures must adhere only to what the general community of doctors customarily do" (p. 76).

When the community standard went out, the "reasonable patient" standard came in. The landmark case was *Canterbury v. Spence* (1972), in which the court found that it is not enough to tell one's patient what other professionals would tell similar patients. For one thing, there might not be a professional consensus for a particular procedure. Further, if the patient is to have a right to self-determination, that right must be set by the law rather than by the community of physicians. Most important, informed consent is founded on the idea of the patient as decision maker. This notion leads to the position taken by the judge in the *Canterbury* case: True consent about what happens to one's self is the informed exercise of a choice; to make that choice, the patient must be given any information about a proposed treatment or its alternatives that a reasonable person in the patient's circumstances would find material to the decision.

The same line of argument has been used in other cases to reinforce the reasonable patient standard. In *Cobbs v. Grant* (1972), the judge said, "It is the prerogative of the patient, not the physician, to determine for himself the direction in which he believes his interests lie" (cited in Pope and

Vasquez, 1991, p. 77). The Canadian Supreme Court took note of the *Canterbury* standard in two 1980 cases. In *Reibl v. Hughes*, the Canadian high court reinforced the primacy of the patient as decision maker and said that in order to make a sound choice the patient must have all the information that the average prudent person, the reasonable person in the patient's particular position, would need.

These legal cases and the ethical codes they have influenced provide a backdrop for consideration of informed consent in psychotherapy.

Psychotherapy, Where Consent Unfolds over Time

Psychotherapy is a process that provides special challenges beyond those we have considered so far. These challenges arise out of some essential features of the process, such as its extension over time, during which views change about the problem and what should be done about it. To appreciate these complexities, consider *Mitchell v. Robinson* (1960). You will recall that a woman suffering from schizophrenia was given insulin and ECT. These caused a convulsion that fractured several vertebrae. The court ruled that she should have been informed of the risk of such physical effects before she consented to the treatment. Note how different this case is from one that involves a course of psychotherapy. There was a clear diagnosis that preceded a discrete intervention (the intervention may have included several sessions of ECT and insulin, but it did not *change* over time).

In psychotherapy, on the other hand, it may be unclear what the client's problems are at the outset—unclear to both therapist and client. A "presenting problem" may change shape over the course of therapy. One problem may be solved, only to have some other problem emerge. The client may decide to change focus. A therapist may come to realize that the problem is not what it seemed to be at the beginning and may recommend such a change in focus. In this book, we will see examples of clients who have been sexually abused in childhood but who come to therapy for treatment of an eating disorder. The earlier abuse may be seen as a factor in the eating disorder or as a separate problem, and the therapist and client may have different opinions about just what is going on.

One of the participants in our study discussed this on going negotiation process. He was a male psychologist working in a university counseling center. His clients often came because they had eating disorders such as bulimia or anorexia, but over the course of therapy other problems became apparent. Here is how he described the situation:

> Informed consent comes through negotiating. You really can't do anything without their active participation and collaboration. You have to agree on what you're working on. But there can be negotiation there, in collaboration with them, encouraging them to change the treatment goals they had in mind when they first came in. (T[9])

As the problem may change during the course of therapy, so may the nature of therapy itself. Psychotherapy involves the building of a relationship, often called a therapeutic alliance; like any relationship, it develops and changes over time. Since the relationship is a component of the treatment (or, in the view of some therapists, essentially *is* the treatment), the intervention also changes over time.

Given these features of psychotherapy, it is evident that it fits poorly into the model of a one-time consent given before the occurrence of some discrete procedure. Therapists may and should, of course, obtain a general consent before starting. There are good consent models to use at the beginning of any therapy with virtually any client (see Everstine et al., 1980). These approaches are necessarily broad and deal with the process in general terms, emphasizing client rights and professional obligations (for example, "You have the right to ask any questions about the procedures used during therapy; if you wish, I shall explain my usual methods to you" [Everstine et al., 1980, p. 832]). But consent regarding *this* client, *this* problem, and *this* intervention must evolve in the course of therapy itself.

If the issues involved in consent evolve during the process, then consent must also evolve. Authors who write about psychotherapy are increasingly calling attention to the fluid nature of the consent practice. Pope and Vasquez say, "As the treatment plan undergoes significant evolution, the patient must adequately understand these changes and voluntarily agree to them" (1991, 75). Evans (1997) recommends, "When a significant change in the treatment or procedure being carried out with a client is contemplated, it is imperative to obtain informed consent for the change" (p. 92). Stone (1990) says, "Informed consent is a process, not an immediate one-time recitation of a formula regardless of the actual situation" (p. 425).

In the present book, I take the view that consent should be renegotiated, however formally or informally, as therapist and client recognize new problems or move in new directions.

How Much Information?

There are three main issues in informed consent, concerning the sort and amount of information that a client needs to make a truly informed decision. These issues are: specific consent; information about alternative treatments; and information about the therapist's conception of the problem and alternative conceptions.

In specific consent, the practitioner tells the client what he or she intends to do and outlines the possible risks and benefits. This is the sort of consent that was the topic of all the court cases referred to earlier; usually, like *Mitchell v. Robinson* (1960), these cases revolved around whether the patient was given adequate information about risks.

There are two main reasons why practitioners sometimes fail to inform clients about risks: Either they do not fully appreciate these risks themselves, or they worry about upsetting the patient. The first is a question of the practitioner's competence; the second has to do with therapeutic privilege, which I discussed earlier. As I noted, the courts are less and less likely to accept therapeutic privilege as a defense offered by a health professional.

Rozovsky and Rozovsky (1990), who are recognized experts on the legal requirements of informed consent, caution professionals against the exercise of therapeutic privilege. In their view, information about a proposed treatment should not be withheld for any of these reasons: it might "upset" the patient; the patient might refuse the treatment on learning of the risks; the patient might not be able to understand the information; or most clinicians would not provide the information. The latter refers, of course, to the abandonment of the reasonable doctor standard.

The second issue in informed consent is whether the practitioner goes beyond talking about his or her proposed treatment and presents alternative treatments to the client. These alternatives may or may not be within the realm of competence of the practitioner; they may require referral elsewhere. The third issue concerns agreement between therapist and client about the presumed causes, or underlying factors, of the client's present problem.

Presentation of alternative treatments is relevant to any intervention. Discussion of underlying factors, on the other hand, is particularly relevant to psychotherapy. It may not be of any importance in proposed lung cancer surgery whether the doctor thinks that smoking causes lung cancer, or whether the patient agrees or disagrees about that. But it is very relevant to psychotherapy whether a therapist treating an eating disorder thinks that such disorders are usually linked to childhood sexual abuse. And it matters whether the therapist's view fits the client's remembered experience.

These two issues—alternative treatments and conceptualization of underlying causes—are discussed more fully in the next two sections.

Presenting Alternatives to the Client

It is increasingly argued that if a client is to make a fully informed decision about whether to have some treatment, he or she ought to know about different treatments that might be available. Even in some of the court cases that revolved around specific consent, judges said that alternatives should be discussed with patients. In *Natanson v. Kline* (1960), where the judge tried to set a standard for the information required in consent, he included possible alternatives. In *Canterbury v. Spence* (1972), the judge said: "True consent to what happens to one's self is the informed exercise of a choice, and that entails an opportunity to evaluate knowledgeably the options available and the risks attendant upon each" (cited in Pope and Vasquez, 1991, p. 77).

Rozovsky and Rozovsky (1990) recommend that, in addition to information about risks and benefits required for specific consent, the practitioner should also give information about reasonable alternatives. Some codes of ethics are also expanding consent to include discussion of alternatives (e.g., Canadian Psychological Association, 1991, Principle I.18).

If there is now some consensus about what ought to be included in specific consent, there is still much controversy about presenting alternatives. In one study, Mahmood (1995) surveyed clinical psychologists and asked about the information they give clients at the outset of therapy. While 91 percent of the respondents informed their patients about the limits of confidentiality, only 65 percent discussed alternative forms of treatment.

One question that arises regarding alternatives is whether one should talk only about the techniques the present therapist can use or whether the discussion should include other forms of therapy that would require a referral. If the latter, then what standard should be used to decide whether such alternatives are "reasonable"? If a treatment is not locally available, or if the therapist believes the client cannot afford it, is there any point in mentioning it?

We found that therapists and clients have a variety of reactions to the question of alternatives, even when they are "reasonable" in the sense of being generally available. Take as an example the question of whether a woman who was sexually abused as a child ought to be told by a male therapist that it might be appropriate for her to be seen by a woman. This issue, which is explored in chapter 5, brought forth various reactions from participants. One client described the way her male therapist suggested a referral:

> He said, "I think you need to work with a woman." I hadn't been over-whelmingly looking for a change. He suggested that I needed a woman's perspective. He said, "You need to be empowered by another woman to get through this." (C[65])

On the other hand, a male psychiatrist was quite disdainful of the notion that a client might ask to be referred to a woman, even though he said he would reluctantly comply:

> "I don't want a male doctor," "I don't want a male psychiatrist," " I don't want a male lawyer," " I don't want a male anything!" "I want" can be self-defeating because you have to deal with the other half of the human race. . . . Some see me and say, "No I don't want to talk to a man about this problem." You just pass them on. It is a consumers' society. More and more, consumers decide what they want, and they're making a mistake and getting nowhere. (T[23])

Some authors believe that presenting alternatives that involve a referral may be interpreted as rejection. "A premature or overly enthusiastic discussion of alternatives may convince the client that the therapist does not want him or her in therapy" (Hare-Mustin et al., 1995, p. 307). We found some support for this concern in our interviews with clients who had been referred. A client who was successfully referred by a male to a female therapist first felt somewhat abandoned: "By suggesting 'somebody else needs to deal with it,' I just felt it was total rejection. I was ready to do the work and he cut me off at the knees."

The importance of discussing alternatives with clients is illustrated by the case of *Osheroff v. Chestnut Lodge*, reported by Packman, Cabot, and Bongar (1994). Osheroff, a physician, was hospitalized at Chestnut Lodge for seven months because of serious family problems and increasing difficulties working with his professional associates. At the Lodge, his symptoms were severe insomnia and incessant pacing. He was treated with intensive psychoanalytic psychotherapy four times a week. His family was concerned that his condition was not improving and in fact was getting worse; for example, during his stay he lost thirty-five pounds.

The family had him discharged and admitted to Silver Hill, where he was treated with antidepressants and phenothiazines. He showed marked improvement within three weeks and was discharged within three months. In 1982 he sued Chestnut Lodge for malpractice, alleging, among other things, that "Chestnut Lodge failed to obtain the informed consent of the patient by failing to disclose to and discuss with him alternative therapeutic modalities and the costs and benefits of each of the alternatives" (Packman, Cabot, and Bongar, 1994, p. 184).

Chestnut Lodge claimed therapeutic privilege: The Lodge's lawyers argued that disclosure of the required information "might have interfered with the treatment process or might have led Dr. Osheroff to refuse consent to the proposed treatment altogether." This defense was rejected by an arbitration panel, which awarded Osheroff $250,000.

Expert witnesses called by Osheroff and Chestnut Lodge disagreed on many things, but they did agree that therapists must give more consideration to presenting alternatives to clients. Gerald Klerman, an expert witness called by Osheroff, said, "The patient has the right to be informed as to the alternatives available, their efficacy, and their likely outcomes." Alan Stone, an expert witness called by Chestnut Lodge, agreed that therapists, including psychoanalysts, should give serious consideration to "presenting patients with information about alternative treatment modalities" (both citations from Packman, Cabot, and Bongar, 1994, p. 188).

In their discussion of the Osheroff case and other recent decisions, Packman, Cabot, and Bongar (1994) recommend (among other things) that "alternative therapeutic modalities must be discussed with patients.

Clinicians can no longer suggest only one form of treatment. Psychotherapists may not be competent in using more than a few treatment approaches; however they should be up-to-date in their knowledge of the standard treatments used by competent, ethical therapists. Futher, they should be able to intelligently explain these options to the patient" (p. 194).

When therapists believe that they should discuss alternatives with their clients, when and how do they do it? What standards do they use to rule out "unreasonable" alternatives? How do they guard against overwhelming the client with indigestible information or making the client feel unwanted? Are they concerned about giving a balanced account of therapy approaches to which they do not subscribe? These are some of the difficult issues surrounding the presentation of alternatives that we explored in interviews with therapists and clients.

Discussing Underlying Factors

Alternative treatments tend to be tied to different ideas about the nature of the client's problem. While such differences may reflect variations in treatment orientation, they may also arise from different notions about the underlying factors that helped create the condition. A therapist may believe such underlying factors have to be dealt with before, or in addition to, the presenting problem.

One of the therapists we interviewed talked about the relationship between eating disorders and childhood sexual abuse. Sometimes an eating disorder brings the client into treatment, but it becomes apparent that there was a history of early abuse. Our participant was one of those who believe that early sexual abuse may be a causal factor in a later eating disorder. If so, the question is whether to focus only on the problem presented by the patient or to try to work on the trauma left over from the early abuse. This therapist, the coauthor of an influential book on feminist therapy, said that she differs from some who prefer to deal with the current problem rather than probing the past:

> I'm one of those people that believes that you have to go back to the source of the trauma. But there are people—including feminist therapists—who would believe in doing just here-and-now work and would find that sufficient. (T[27])

This view, that one must go to the "source of the trauma," can be compared with that of another of our participants. He was a psychologist in a university counseling center who saw many female students with eating disorders. Although he believed there were underlying causes that could be worked on, he was comfortable dealing with the behavior itself, if that was what the client wanted:

> If they say, "Well, I just wanted to focus on changing this particular type of behavior"—it doesn't hurt people to work on reducing their bingeing. So even though I think that it's not all we can do, or even the most beneficial thing we can do, in the final analysis I still believe it is beneficial. Let's just work on that; we'll just limit to that and we'll see how it goes. I think that it may not be sufficient, but I'm willing to give it a try, and I tell them, "Look, if it works out well, and it's fine for you, and you just eliminate that behavior and that's all you want to do, that's fine." (T[9])

With regard to the contract about which problem ought to be addressed, he said the therapist-client relationship was no different from relationships in other professions. He made the analogy to a discussion between a garage mechanic and a car owner:

> You take your car to a garage and the mechanic can say, "Well, you know it's making this noise, and this isn't working," and then they say, "By the way this, this, and this you could have this done, too." And you say, "Yeah, well, that's nice, but I think I'll let it go." The mechanic might be right in the judgment that it's better to deal with that now rather than later—that it will cause you problems later. "That's fine, but that's not where I'm at right now." And that's okay. (T[9])

These therapists clearly have different approaches to the issue of whether to go beyond the client's presenting problem, or how much to encourage the client to do so.

There is an emerging legal basis for discussing the therapist's belief about the client's problem and its causes as part of a comprehensive consent process. That was evident in *Osheroff v. Chestnut Lodge*. Earlier, I pointed to this case as an example of the importance of discussing alternative treatments. But different treatments are usually aimed at solving different problems. Chestnut Lodge and Silver Hill saw the problem differently, and that was the basis for their preference for different treatments.

Chestnut Lodge, which had a strong psychoanalytic orientation, believed Osheroff was suffering from narcissistic personality disorder. This view was based not on his present behavior, such as incessant pacing to the point where his feet blistered and bled; it was based on his previous history, primarily his difficult relationships with other people. Silver Hill treated him with a combination of antidepressants and phenothiazines because they thought he was suffering from psychotic depressive reaction, based primarily on their view of his current symptoms.

The issue is not which institution was right—they could both have been right. The issue is the failure to discuss these possibilities with the patient in the consent process. Chestnut Lodge held staff meetings in which there were debates about disclosing more information to Osheroff; staff decided against it because discussion with him might play into his supposed personality disorder.

In the study reported in this book, I focused on three problem areas about which there is considerable disagreement over underlying factors. In eating disorders such as anorexia and bulimia, there are a wide variety of available treatment approaches, all based on somewhat different conceptions of the causal factors. There is a major controversy among those who treat survivors of childhood sexual abuse: some advocate the uncovering of repressed memories, and others worry about false memory syndrome. Practitioners who work with sex offenders face questions about the role of sexual abuse that the offender may have suffered and the capacity of offenders for developing empathy. All these divergent views can, in theory, be a focus of ongoing consent negotiations.

Therapy Narratives in Consent

Like other stories, therapy narratives have a beginning, middle, and end. "Underlying factors" belong to the beginning of the narrative, the presumed source of the problem that is the focus of therapy. Howard (1991) has referred to life as the stories we live by, and to psychotherapy as exercises in story repair. To repair the story, therapist and client have to agree at some point on what the story is. And that, I would argue, requires discussion and eventual agreement about origins.

To what extent should therapist and client share the same narrative? At the outset of therapy they may not, but during the process they must either come closer, or therapy becomes frustrating and the client tunes out or walks away. There is probably some range of difference that works. If they are too far apart, they live in different worlds. But if they are in complete agreement from the outset, there may be no impetus for change. Social psychological studies have established that there is more attitude change the farther apart two people are, but only up to a certain point. When they are too far away, there is a boomerang effect, and the message is simply ignored (King, 1975). In studies of therapy, too, there is evidence that the process is affected by the assumptions that clients and therapists bring to the situation (Hacking, 1991; Highlen and Hill, 1984; Lyddon, 1989).

In successful therapy, there is a natural coming together over time between therapist and client as long as they are, at the outset, willing to listen each other's accounts. The therapist brings expertise and experience with a range of more or less similar cases. The client knows his or her own life events. Over time, the therapist's view of the way things generally happen will be modified *by and for* this case. And, over time, the client's understanding of what has happened to him or her will be modified by the therapist's perspective.

Returning to the issue of consent, we find that one of the matters on which a therapist-client pair needs to have roughly similar views is on choice and control of the therapeutic process. When accounts differ, how are they to be reconciled? Is one narrative privileged over the other—because it is "my story" or because "I am the expert"? In our interviews, there are stories of therapy that failed because no way was found to reconcile different narratives, as well as stories of therapy that succeeded because the gap was bridged between the way two people saw the world.

2

■ ■　■　■　■　　■　　　■　　　■　　　　■

Asking Questions

HERE IS A QUESTION asked in one of our interviews. It came a third of the way through a one-hour interview conducted in a prison with a psychologist who treats sex offenders. The inmates volunteer for such treatment, the psychologist has just said, and they cannot be made to participate against their will.

> *Interviewer:* I guess one of the obvious questions is the difference between a client who is participating with free will because they have chosen to pursue a therapeutic intervention and incarcerated persons who are in need of therapy but the choice is no longer theirs. [Mutual acquaintance] and I talked a little bit about this, and he explained to me that in a sense it is volunteer because they are not forced to participate; but then in a sense they are not really volunteers because it is usually part of their rehabilitation, is that . . . ?

The issue the interviewer has raised is about free and informed consent. Such consent has been a sine qua non of ethical research with humans, as discussed in chapter 1, at least since the Nuremberg war crimes trials and development of the Nuremberg Code.

As the conversational style of the question indicates, our interviewers did not work from scripts. Marianne Paget, who uses a similar interview method, has commented, "Specific, spontaneously constructed, and contextually sensitive questions . . . are characteristic of in-depth interviews. Rather than being impediments to the creation of reliable knowledge, they show how knowledge is actually created" (1983, p. 73).

We will return to the sample question in a moment. First, though, to understand the role of any separate question in an interview, what it might elicit and what the participant might make of it, we need to know what the participant — and the interviewer, for that matter — thought the interview was about.

In preliminary contact, interviewers discussed the project with potential participants. It was established that therapists specialized in one or more of three areas: treating those with eating disorders, sexual abuse survivors, or sex offenders. (Sometimes we knew this information before the initial contact.) Specific problem areas were chosen because there might be informed consent issues associated with the problem itself, such as the battle for control that many see in anorexia, the need to establish trust for survivors of sexual abuse, and the constraints imposed by the legal system in treatment of sex offenders.

Participants were then told that we wanted to do a rather open interview about their therapy. I was identified as the principal researcher, and my interest in ethical issues was communicated (in some cases it was already known by the participant). The interviewer said there would be questions about the way the therapist handled informed consent and about negotiating consent in the therapist's problem area.

Each interview began with questions about how the therapist got into this particular field (therapy in general, and the therapist's area of specialization). Therapists talked about their backgrounds, including the aspirations or accidents that led them to their present work. The interviewer asked about the therapist's preferred treatment, about other available treatments, and about communication of such matters with the client.

We interviewed ninety-two people. Therapists came from a wide variety of professions, including psychology, psychiatry, social work, nursing, and occupational therapy, and some gave themselves other designations, such as holistic therapist or bioenergetic therapist.

Twenty of the interviewees were clients or former clients who also fell into the three problem domains. We gave clients the same general information, with less emphasis on informed consent and more on learning about their experience of psychotherapy. Some clients were referred by therapists; others learned about the project and volunteered.

All interviews took place at a site of the participant's choosing. They lasted about an hour and were tape recorded and later transcribed. Identities were kept confidential.

The interviewers knew they had certain areas to cover: background information, treatment preference and alternatives, opinions and practices with regard to consent, and ideas about the etiology of the condition. The interviewer generally covered the topics in that order. It was most natural, for instance, to get acquainted by asking about the participant's background before moving to topics such as style of therapy and views of consent. Interviewers were free to ask follow-up questions.

The structure tended to be more elastic when clients were interviewed. Although we wanted to know about their experience of informed consent, for example, we knew that most clients would not have a body of information attached to the word "consent," as therapists typically did. What they had to say about consent was elicited by asking general questions about their therapy experience, with follow-up questions that touched on whether they were given options, how those were presented, whether they felt they were on the same wave length as their therapists concerning the cause of their problem, and so on. We also asked clients if they would like to have been treated differently, in what way, and, in particular, what choices they would like to have had in therapy.

During the interviews, we were interested in anything the participant chose to talk about. We did not want the interviews to be driven entirely by our agenda, and, indeed, they were not. Participants offered many opinions and accounts we had not anticipated.

Here is an example of the emergence of the unexpected: We interviewed (separately) a client and her previous and current therapists. We knew that the previous therapist, a man, had transferred the female client to a female colleague. We understood this was a successful transfer; the client told us her male therapist explained that his colleague did feminist therapy, which he felt would benefit the client at that point in her treatment. When we interviewed the referring therapist, however, we were surprised to hear a diatribe against feminists, feminist theory, and feminist therapists (see chapter 5). The crucial role of surprises and anomalies in qualitative research will be discussed in chapter 3. The point here is that our interview style is intended to leave lots of room for the unexpected.

This, then, is the general interview context in which the above question was asked.

The Sample Question

Now let's examine the question with which I opened this chapter more closely. It touches on a topic that the therapist already knew, from preliminary contact, would be a focus of the interview. The question is framed to reflect a consent issue that might well arise in a prison setting.

In this style of interviewing, the questions are often reflective, intended to open the dialogue to a thoughtful interchange. This almost always worked. In our later examination of all transcripts, we found only two (both therapists rather than clients) in which the participant seemed guarded throughout.

In the sample question, the interviewer offers two opposing points of view about the consent issue with regard to prisoners. She first offers a contrast between someone not in prison who makes the choice to come for therapy and an "incarcerated person," who, she speculates, has no choice. But then she refers to someone that both she and the participant know—someone else working in the prison system—and quotes him as suggesting that the contrast may not be as sharply drawn as it appears. The other therapist had told her that inmates do not have to participate in treatment programs, so any who do so are exercising choice. She suggests, in the thinking-aloud manner that our interviewers tended to use (because, in fact, they were thinking aloud), that perhaps those who volunteer are not "really" volunteers because treatment is a recognized part of the rehabilitation program for sex offenders. A host of issues are implied by this comment, including the possible coercion created by the need for prisoners to be cooperative in order to win parole, and so on. These are matters than could be explored as the conversation unfolds. I present and discuss the answer to the question in chapter 3. Now, more about interviewing.

The Research Interview as Focused Conversation

My approach to research interviewing is not new. It was outlined by the outstanding social scientist Paul Lazarsfeld (1972) in a paper called "The Art of Asking Why," originally published in 1936 in an obscure, now-defunct marketing journal. Lazarsfeld emphasized the need for flexibility in asking questions in a research interview. One must fit questions to the experience of the participant. Lazarsfeld pointed out that this style conflicts with the tradition that a question should be so worded as always to have precisely the same effect on all those interviewed.

In contrast, he advocated what he called a loose and liberal handing of questions by an interviewer. The meaning is more important than the wording, and much depends on the sophistication of the interviewer. Lazarsfeld's approach requires the interviewer to have "the responsibility for knowing exactly what he is trying to discover, and permits him to vary the wording in accordance with the experience of the respondent" (p. 193).

The interviewer must be adept at asking "why" questions. In the sample given, answers would be followed up by further questions such as, "Why do you think that?" or, "Why do you do that?" A "why" question can elicit many reasons, only some of which are relevant. The question "Why do you do that" could be answered with reasons like "Because they pay me to do it" or "Because it works." Much depends on the way in which the interviewer and participant understand what is going on, and therefore what sort of reason makes sense in the conversational context.

Lazarsfeld noted that asking for reasons and giving answers are commonplace habits of everyday life. We are used to asking "why" questions, and we are seldom disappointed in the answers, because someone we engage in conversation usually knows which of many possible reasons is relevant. "He picks out the reason which he hopes will contribute especially to a mutual understanding of the present situation" (p. 183). A major task for the interviewer is to create a climate in which there will be that mutual understanding.

One of many reasons why our style of interviewing avoids a script is the need to pose sensitive follow-up questions. These have to flow from the twists and turns of ongoing dialogue. When asking "why" questions, for example, the interviewer must be aware—at least intuitively—of two aspects of an answer that, in Lazarsfeld's terms, correspond to *attributes* and *influences*. "Why" questions are usually answered first with reference to an attribute; further probing is needed to focus on an influence. For instance, the question "Why do you think people volunteer for your treatment program?" is usually answered first with an attribute such as "Because it helps them" or "Because they think it helps them." A follow-up question can be directed to the attribute aspect of the answer, such as, "In what way does it help them?" It can also be directed to the influence aspect: "Why do you think it helps them?" Or, "Why do *they* think it helps them?"

The ongoing conversational context determines how the participant interprets and answers questions. Lazarsfeld made this point by quoting a remark from G. K. Chesterton's *The Invisible Man*: "People never answer what you say, they answer what you mean or what they think you mean" (cited in Lazarsfeld, 1972, p. 195).

Lazarsfeld formulated a "principle of tacit assumption" to explain how interviewer and participant manage to coordinate their moves in conversation. If our interviewer asks about a particular therapeutic procedure—"Why do you do that?"—the answer is unlikely to be "Because they pay me," since both parties tacitly assume that sort of thing. Even "Because it works" would generally be assumed; therapists try something only if they think it will work. If the interviewer and the participant are working with compatible tacit assumptions, the answer will probably be a more detailed rationale.

Here is an illustration from our study of the way questions and answers work on a foundation of tacit assumptions. The interviewers asked several therapists why they used group therapy rather than individual treatment. When we asked the question of some therapists who work with sex offenders in groups, they told us that sex offenders are manipulative and need the sort of confrontation that they get in a group. When we asked the same question of a therapist who ran groups for people with eating disorders, he told us there were not enough resources to see clients individually, whether or not individual therapy might sometimes be more productive. His clinic had a long waiting list, and it was necessary to use groups in order to see as many people as possible. These are different sorts of answers, but they probably involve the same tacit assumption. In the first case, therapists told us why they thought group treatment was best. In the second case, the therapist told us why consideration of "the best treatment" had been overtaken by financial constraints. In neither case was there any need to talk about the tacit assumption that therapists would use the "best" treatment if they could.

An Emerging Body of Work in Psychology

This book is part of a series of monographs designed to showcase the qualitative approach in psychology. The series is an acknowledgment of two facts: first, that psychology has much less experience with qualitative methods than other disciplines, such as sociology and medicine; and, second, that there are psychologists who are actively engaged in qualitative research. We are seeing what Kidder (1982) has called a new emphasis in psychology on listening to the stories people have to tell. Kvale (1992) refers to it as a conversational turn: "The qualitative research interview is no longer a mere adjunct to the basic scientific methods of observation and experimentation but provides, through a conversation between persons, privileged access to the cultural world of intersubjective meaning" (p. 51).

I am presenting, then, a study that fits into an emerging body of work in psychology that uses qualitative methods—research interviews, in particular. I would like to give some illustrations of the sorts of questions psychologists are exploring with these methods. Here are four examples.

James Garbarino and Claire Bedard (cited in Garbarino, 1997) used long and detailed interviews, conducted at two youth prisons in New York State, with violent youthful offenders to construct narrative accounts of their lives. Participants included young people incarcerated for murder and other severe acts of violence.

Their work was aimed, first, at giving voice to these young offenders who consistently told interviewers that no one had ever asked them to tell their story before. The researchers believed that all violence makes sense if one looks with open eyes and listens with an open heart and mind, and they called their study "Making Sense of Senseless Youth Violence."

Their second objective was to give narrative coherence to the experience of the young, violent offenders. They define narrative coherence as a way of connecting events into a life story, in a way that gives meaning to events. They contend that the effect of early events on later outcomes is determined primarily by the quality of the narrative account that one can develop, the story one can tell of one's life.

The second example is another study of urban adolescents, this time not violent youth in prisons but twenty-four teenagers trying to succeed, and to define success, in a difficult urban environment. I refer to Niobe Way's (1998) study of urban teenagers, *Everyday Courage*.

Way, a developmental psychologist, wanted to learn from a group of young people what it takes to cope with the daily challenges presented by growing up in the inner city. She knew that psychologists usually generalize to this group (and all adolescents) on the basis of middle-class samples. She knew, too, that our popular understanding of these young people is often based on negative stereotypes from media accounts. But she believed there was much to be gained from listening to the voices of a cross-section of urban teenagers who want to make positive change in their lives and communities even as they struggle with concerns about racism and violence.

The third example is from a study of feminist therapy by Jeanne Marecek and Diane Kravetz (1998). They did one hundred interviews with women and men therapists and counselors, all of whom considered themselves to be feminists and to bring a feminist perspective to their practice.

The interviews lasted an hour or two and consisted of broad, open-ended questions about feminism in therapy, with probes for specific examples. They were interested in looking at shared language practices; in other words, what do feminist therapists actually have in common? They examined the way these therapists constructed accounts of their work.

The work of Marecek and Kravetz is timely, because it will appear as various groups consider whether there should be specialty recognition for feminist psychology practice. This would entail codification of practices and principles, standards for training, and so on. Marecek and Kravitz found, however, that a uniform standard of feminist practice would be nearly impossible to achieve. What is called feminist therapy involves a multiplicity of ideas about principles, processes, and therapy goals.

The final example is the work of Malcolm Westcott (1988, 1992, 1994), who uses research interviews to study human freedom. He has been looking at the topic for more than twenty years, in what he calls a progressively evolving fashion. "I began with interviews, moved on to more traditional questionnaire studies, and, dissatisfied with aggregate data, I have returned to interviews and a narrative approach" (1994, p. 160).

He tells potential informants that the interviews are oriented around three questions: What sort of role does freedom play in your life? Are there times when you feel or have felt especially free? What, if anything, do you do to enhance your feeling of freedom?

Westcott's research led him to conclude that human freedom in contemporary Western society lies in the making of committed choices in keeping with one's conception of one's nature, accepting responsibility for those choices and their consequences, and pursuing some degree of perfection in a chosen realm. Such a conception allows for a great variety of concrete practices, from the creation of a new persona to the maximization of privacy to commitment and service to family. In his book *The Psychology of Human Freedom,* he explains that freedom is both an abstract concept and a concrete lived human experience: "To seek a psychological understanding of human freedom without attention to the lived experience is meaningless" (1988, p. 163).

These four illustrations indicate the range of questions that psychologists are exploring, using what are, in our field, nontraditional methods. Many other examples could have been chosen, such as Carol Gilligan's (1991) work in the Harvard Project on the psychology of women.

I indicated earlier that other disciplines have a head start in qualitative work, and researchers outside psychology have been studying a host of interesting issues using interviews, oral histories, and the like. I mention only a few: Marianne Paget (1983), who interviewed women artists about the meaning of art in their lives; Elliot Mishler (1986a, 1986b), who interviewed husbands and wives about marital relationships at midlife; Kathy Charmaz (1994), who interviewed people with chronic illnesses to learn about their situations, perspectives, and identity dilemmas; and Studs Terkel, who captured firsthand narratives about work, about the Great Depression, and about the American dream (1970, 1972, 1988).

You will have noticed that the questions that impel qualitative research seem to be structured differently from the hypothesis testing that is traditional in psychology. This matter is discussed in chapter 3.

A Note on Presentation

There are two basic approaches to presenting interview material. The first is to present transcripts, or parts of transcripts, as close to what the typist heard as possible, with all the redundancies, groping for words, the pauses, the "ums" and "ahs", and so on. The second approach is to smooth the rough edges so that what the person is trying to say becomes easier to understand. The choice depends upon the form of analysis—primarily *discourse analysis* or *theme analysis*. I discuss these different sorts of analysis in a moment. First, here is an example from our study showing the different styles of presenting data. It is taken from a section of transcript between interviewer EC and a therapist who has just been asked if she talks about various treatment options with clients:

T^3: I'm not sure that I am quite with you on what you're alluding to as the choice of treatments. Because my own approach is largely, I would say almost exclusively, cognitive behavioral.

EC: Um-hmm.

T^3: And I can apply that whether the issue we're working on is self-esteem or if it's monitoring, ah, what you're going to be choosing in the dining hall this week, or how you're dealing with your residence, friends, your friends in residence.

EC: Um-hmm.

T^3: Umm. So, my approach [pause] doesn't differ that much I think. I think that's what I'm saying.

EC: Yeah. Okay. And so then, basically, you would—how do you approach that then with the client? Do you outline the sort of things you're going to work with them on and how do you engage them in this process?

T^3: Yeah. That's a good question. [sigh] I think it's really important to engage them in the first session.

EC: Um-hmm.

T^3: And I do that as part of my orientation as to who I am and what my approach is and what I see us doing together, if we're going to work together. And I give the whole choice to them from the very beginning. Whether they choose to come back or not is, is in their ballpark.

EC: Um-hmm.

T^3: I can, you know, and I will make recommendations that I feel that this will be a good experience, but the bottom line is that it needs to be their choice.

EC: Um-hmm, Um-hmm.

T^3: And, umm, you know, and I have them go both ways. Some do and some don't come back.

I would transform that piece of raw material into a more readable narrative. It would look like this:

> My own approach is largely, I would say almost exclusively, cognitive-behavioral. I can apply that whether the issue we're working on is self-esteem or whether it's monitoring what the client is going to be choosing to eat in the dining hall this week, or how they're dealing with their friends in residence.
>
> My approach doesn't differ that much from client to client.
>
> I think it's really important to engage clients in the first session. I do that as part of my orientation as to who I am and what my approach is and what I see us doing together, if we're going to work together. And I give the whole choice to them from the very beginning. Whether they choose to come back or not is in their ballpark. I can and I will make recommendations that I feel that this will be a good experience, but the bottom line is that it needs to be their choice. I have them go both ways. Some do and some don't come back. (T^3)

Much is gained by the process of smoothing. The participant's voice is clearer without the distractions that occur when one is trying to think aloud. This smoothing is used by, among others, Terkel (1970, 1972, 1988) in his famous oral histories, by Charmaz (1994) in her study of chronically ill men, by Laidlaw, Malmo, and associates (1990) in their book on feminist therapy, and by Gilligan (1982) in her work on moral development in women.

If much is gained, is anything lost? That depends on what analysis is being used, and for what purpose. In *discourse analysis* it is essential to have the transcript as close to what was actually said as possible. The researcher who uses this approach does not have the luxury of deliberately smoothing talk, because discourse analysis focuses on language—the way things are said—much more than on *what* is said. McMullen's (1989) work on metaphor in therapy is an example of the valuable lessons one can learn from close reading of the way people express themselves.

Tannen (1989) offers an excellent introduction to the uses of discourse analysis in her book *Talking Voices*. She notes that, although it is a heterogeneous group of methods used by researchers from a variety of disciplines, discourse analysis is fundamentally a subdiscipline of linguistics. In her own use of discourse analysis, for instance, Tannen focuses on "how repetition, dialogue and imagery create involvement in discourse" (p. 9). But a focus on how people talk is quite different from studying what they are actually talking about.

The present study employs *theme analysis*. Here the concern is with *what* is being said, rather than the form of words used to say it. As Paget (1983) explains, this sort of research requires the interviewer and the analyst to be "continuously caring about the meaning of what is being said" (p. 87). Mishler (1986b) notes that interview participants explain things in stories, and the analyst's central question is always: What is the story about?

Westcott (1992, 1994) describes how he smoothes interviews to make their meaning clear without loss of authenticity. He folds his questions into the answers and deletes redundancy. His aim is to present a coherent personal narrative. Westcott does not, however, drain speech of its richness; he leaves the speaker's style intact, including profanity, metaphor, and personal examples.

Seidman (1991), in *Interviewing as Qualitative Research,* says it is essential to reduce and then shape the material into a form in which it can be shared or displayed. He points out that the researcher has already decided to present some portions of transcripts and not others. Leaving the selected portions in raw form may give the illusion that nothing is left out, but it is an illusion. Spence (1986) makes a similar point: There are inevitable smoothing processes that occur no matter how rough the transcript may appear. Grice (1989) has identified conversational maxims that we all use in everyday conversations to make them coherent and comprehensible. If we use these strategies to understand one another in everyday life, why not employ them to make interviews clear?

Here is a final example of the smoothing process as I use it in this book. This time I eliminate the interviewer and just show how a small section of conversation is smoothed into the form in which it will be presented (see chapter 5). This is a therapist talking about the relationship between being a feminist and setting fees for therapy. In the raw transcript data, presented first, all her fumbling about for words, her false starts, and her pauses are left in.

> And ah I put that in the context of feminism: that you know we are—ah that [Pause] I am just trying to think of the—it's almost pretty well pattern. [Pause] Uhm part of being a feminist is the commitment that ah people should have choices in all areas of their life including therapy and ah I don't like ah—if people come into therapy, it is usually because they have some difficulties to work out. I don't want the cost of therapy to add to those difficulties.

Here is version two:

> I put that in the context of feminism: Part of being a feminist is the commitment that people should have choices in all areas of their life including therapy. If people come into therapy, it is usually because they have some difficulties to work out. I don't want the cost of therapy to add to those difficulties. (T^{63})

I contend that the second version cleans away the distractions while losing nothing of the meaning that the therapist was trying to convey.

3

■ ■ ■ ■ ■ ■ ■ ■

Making Meaning

WE ASKED a psychologist who worked with sex offenders in prison was asked what "uncoerced consent" means for inmates who volunteer for his program. I began chapter 2 with the question; I begin this one with his answer. It will serve as a starting point for a discussion of the approach to qualitative analysis taken in this book.

> It's a question of how much freedom, free choice do you have in that kind of an environment. [Offenders] are in the context of a prison. They have, in that context, freedom of choice to say "I'm not gonna do this" or "I'm not gonna do that."
>
> I guess in a sense it is the same thing in society. How much free will do we have in certain circumstances out here to say "Yes, I will do that" or "I won't do that"? It's more constrained, and there are certain benefits in saying yes. In some cases, it's going to be to "reduce my time in prison by saying yes." But it may *increase* my time in prison, as with the guy that is going to the police now with more disclosures. Or, I may not do very well in the program, so I'm not gonna get a good recommendation.
>
> Guys come into the program and say, "Okay, I'm gonna do this for the parole." It's legitimate. But if he is just gonna come here and sit and not do anything, that's not gonna be very beneficial to him.

You are going to do something if it's going to benefit you. On average it does, [but] we get some guys who have done very well in the program but are considered, for various reasons, by the parole board too high a risk to get released. These guys have really done a lot better than other guys, but the conditions of the release are safer, supposedly, for this guy who hasn't done very well; his family may have split up, so there may not be a potential victim. We have had that a lot, where the other inmates can see guys have done real well, and when they hit the parole board they may get denied. And what they are saying is, "Well, why should we do the program?"

The idea of the program is not just to put people through and put a stamp on them; we are really after some depth in personal change. And the interesting thing is there is enough of a community there of people who have been through the program, and some of them have been refused [parole], yet are still very supportive.

And we have inmates coming into the prison—and it's a word-of-mouth thing in a lot of cases—saying, "Look, it's a good thing to do." There's a milieu that's been built there over six years with inmates and with staff that make it something. And we use guys who have been through as facilitators in the program. Right now we've got two guys we've used as facilitators a couple of times and have done really well. They have not been able to get out, and they are initiating a support group within the prison now for sex offenders. (T[43])

This answer can be analyzed at three levels, with increasing interpretation and abstraction at each level. First, the speaker's words (edited and organized) may be presented without paraphrase—the so-called literal level. At the second level, the researcher applies some overt interpretation about what the speaker "means," while staying close to contextual features of the case. At the third level, the analysis is more abstract, making generalizations that go across cases. At each level, we gain something and lose something; I argue for a style of analysis that oscillates among these three levels.

Three Levels of Analysis

The literal level is represented in oral history and oral biography as done by people like George Plimpton (1997) and Studs Terkel (1970, 1972, 1988). Interpretation is limited to deciding what parts of an interview to include and how interview material should be arranged. This is not mere presentation of so-called raw data, although it may seem so to the reader and, because of that, gain considerable rhetorical power. The selection and placement of extracts from various voices creates a mosaic; the ordering can, if the author chooses, construct a tight narrative, as in Plimpton's (1997) study of Truman Capote's involvement with the murder case that led to the book *In Cold Blood*.

The second level shows more overt interpretation, while staying close to the material. The reader goes beyond the words, asking what the answer implies. But the answer is still what Geertz (1983) calls "local knowledge," an answer in context. In the present example, it is the answer of a psychologist working in a prison talking about the ethical notion of consent in answer to a question about what free choice might mean *in this setting* and the motives inmates might have to volunteer for a therapy program. Treating the sample answer in this way, what sorts of things can be said?

We can see that the question the interviewer raised is important to the psychologist. This is apparent from the evident promptness and the amount of detail in his answer. The psychologist probably recognized long before the interview that the issue of uncoerced consent, when one is treating a prison population, constituted a problem to be solved. Whether or not an issue is important to the participant can be interesting in itself. One of the striking findings in Julie Wong's (1989) study of a motion picture censor board was the extent to which the censors had *not* thought about questions that were, in theory, an important part of their mandate, such as the perceived artistic value of a film.

Returning to the sample answer from the prison psychologist, we see that the detail and the repetition of ideas suggest that the solution to the problem of uncoerced consent is not an easy one. The psychologist does not rely on any simple formulation such as, inmates lose rights in prison and coercion is part of the package. Instead, he marshals arguments to support his position that prisoners are not really treated substantially differently from other citizens with respect to consent. He gives examples to indicate that prisoners are free to chose within a context, and he makes the more general argument that there are constraints on all our choices.

With regard to reward as constraint, he takes it as a given that "you are going to do something if it's going to benefit you." Again, the examples and the amount of detail suggest that this is not a facile resolution. He has had to think over the arguments to develop a position that is consistent with inmates consenting to treatment while motivated by parole. He has several rationales for his position that this is not coercive. For example, he suggests, their motivation is their own business as long as they actually work in the treatment group. He notes, too, that some wind up serving longer terms, like one inmate whose treatment prompted him to disclose further offenses to the police. He argues that inmates have just as much reason to think it will damage their record if they do not "do very well in the program" as they have to think that participating in treatment will look good. Finally, he points to cases in which group members who have been denied parole, probably contrary to their expectation, have nevertheless continued to support the group and even to become facilitators.

The third level of analysis is more abstract, with fewer features of the actual answer included in the interpretation. This analysis attempts to strip away some contextual features so that the interpretations are more general; they can be applied, to some extent, across contexts. Kathy Charmaz (1983) calls this step going from substantive to theoretical categories. Here is some level-three analysis of the psychologist's answer; he might be interpreted as saying:

> I accept the ethical principle that people should receive psychological treatment only if their consent is uncoerced. But the fact that there are constraints on choice does not necessarily amount to coercion. All our choices are made in some constraining context. Prisoners may volunteer because they expect that it will look good on their record. People on the outside *also* work within reward systems that influence their choices, and if that is not coercion on the outside, neither is it coercion in prison. The fact that people do what they perceive to be in their own interest does not mean they are not free. People have different interests; they may do something for one sort of reward and find that, in the process, they gain another reward that is more gratifying and more lasting.

As the level of analysis becomes more general, it both gains and loses something. In this case, what is gained is a way to talk about more fundamental processes, such as how people think about free will and about the morality of doing something because you expect to get something out of it. Abstractions may refer to the consent process in general or to the place of reward in free choice, without being tied to treatment of sex offenders in a prison.

What is lost in "context stripping" (Guba and Lincoln, 1994, p. 106) is the grounding of abstract concepts in a real situation. As categories of explanation are made more abstract, they risk becoming detached from anyone's lived experience—just as a statistical average may not fit a single member of the sample (the average family has 1.9 children, but no family has 1.9 children). In the interview response analyzed here, the abstractions leave behind the detail of how a therapist thinks about consent in relation to his work with sex offenders in prison.

The solution to the problem of gaining generality at the cost of losing lived experience is to move back and forth among the three levels during the analysis of qualitative data. In this oscillation, the researcher presents actual voices, albeit within a mosaic that is created by the researcher's notion of what is important to the topic; the researcher also presents an understanding of the participant's viewpoint and from time to time attempts general statements about the topic at hand, such as negotiation of consent in psychotherapy. Louise Kidder and Michelle Fine (1997) capture these analytic moves in the evocative phrase "dancing with the data" (p. 38).

In his book on interviewing, Seidman (1991) notes that there is a temptation to stop at the first level, to let the interviews speak for themselves. In a sense, that is what writers of oral histories try to do. But the data never speak for themselves. In interviews, for example, the answer is always a response to some question. Using Bakhtin's (1981) term, questions and answers are dialogic. Participants interpret questions on the basis of their personal knowledge about similar questions; they frame their responses according to the reactions they hope to produce or the impression they want to make. Further, when responses are selected and organized for presentation, shaping the reader's perception of them, there is another dialogic relationship—this time, between researcher and an imagined reader.

In moving from the literal level, the researcher is accepting what Fine (1996) calls *interpretive authority*—taking a stand with the data. She warns that there is a risk in "the romanticizing of narratives and the concomitant retreat from analysis" (Fine, 1994, p. 80).

In any event, most qualitative researchers feel the job is not done unless and until they have tried to say what they learned from the interviews. In Seidman's words, we want to examine and talk about such questions as: "What connections are there among the experiences of the participants?

What surprises have there been? What confirmations of previous instincts? How have interviews been consistent with the literature? How inconsistent? How have they gone beyond?" (1991, p. 102). These sorts of questions guide the treatment of data in this book.

Interpretation of interviews requires some judgment about whose words are taken at face value, and how do we decide whose words to accept? The answer depends on what Fine refers to as a triple representational problem: Who am I? How do I present the people I have interviewed? How do I treat the people my participants are talking about?

Consider, once again, the psychologist talking about free choice in a prison setting. Fine's triple representational problem involves my own ideas about, among other things, what constitutes freedom of choice (in general, and in the consent process): It involves an interpretation of what the respondent says about such issues, and it involves thinking about how the psychologist presents the sex offenders, those who are not interviewed but only described.

I now move from the illustration—the prison psychologist's response—to some general ideas about qualitative analysis that inform the treatment of interview data in this book.

Qualitative Analysis

Different psychologies present different pictures of people—as behaving organisms, as computer-like programs, and so on. The sort of psychology that underlies this book is that articulated by Jerome Bruner when he said, "The central concept of a human psychology is *meaning* and the processes and transactions involved in the construction of meanings" (1990, p. 33). In a psychology that emphasizes meaning, the central question is: How do people organize their pasts, presents, and anticipated futures so that their life stories are personally coherent? The task of the researcher is, to borrow Kermode's phrase, "to make sense of the ways we make sense of the world" (1967, p. 31).

Qualitative analysis is a somewhat more self-conscious version of the meaning-making in which we all engage throughout our lives. An adequate method must do justice to the way people think, the contexts of their action, and the way they communicate about important issues (O'Neill and Trickett, 1982). The interview method should, in principle, meet these criteria. That is, it should be suited to the enterprise of asking what people think they do and why they think they do it.

I take my emphasis on meaning in context from the work of anthropologist Clifford Geertz (1973, 1983), who says that we live in webs of signification we ourselves have spun. He borrows from the philosopher Gilbert Ryle a contrast between thin and thick description. Thin description tries to strip away the situated meanings of human behavior. Such analysis, Geertz says, risks losing touch with the hard surfaces of life. Thick description, on the other hand, retains the multiple inferences and implications of that behavior. It is the attempt to describe particular attempts by particular people to put important issues in a meaningful frame.

My notion of oscillating among levels from the words of the participant to thick description and then to more general statements implies that there is something to be gained from abstractions. While contexts provide the unique aspects of experience, only abstractions permit comparison of cases across categories, helping us understand generic processes. As we move from what we know and try to generalize our abstractions, our work is necessarily more tentative and speculative. Howard Becker (1992) points out that a major problem in any form of social research is reasoning from the parts we know to something about the whole we do not fully know. This is not the sort of sampling problem one finds in quantitative research. Rather, it involves making inferences about what the whole must be like for this part to be what it is, or what the whole story would have to be for this step to occur as it did.

Themes and Variations

In chapter 2, when I talked about interview style, I referred to theme analysis to distinguish my work from discourse or textual analysis. I might also call it analysis of themes and variations, since the focus is not only on the main themes that emerge but on variations—exceptional cases that enrich emerging ideas by their apparent contrariness. This analysis of negative cases is in stark contrast to the usual quantitative methods of hypothesis-testing research. In that paradigm, unusual cases are relegated to the wastebasket category of "error variance." Worse, they may be dismissed completely from the analysis, losing even error-variance status, because they are considered to be the dreaded "outlyers"—people whose responses are so extreme that they must have misunderstood the researcher's question or instructions. (*Webster's Third* quotes the philosopher of science S. C. Pepper's definition of outlyers: "facts which might not corroborate the facts already organized by the structural hypothesis" [1981, p. 1602]).

In presenting her method of *theory elaboration*, Diane Vaughn (1992) points out that the qualitative researcher works toward not only greater specificity but also greater ambiguity. Specificity refers to determining the limits of applicability of some theoretical notion. Ambiguity helps us go beyond what we thought we knew when we started. Analysis of qualitative data has the potential to show, in Vaughn's words, "intricate, interconnected detail, much of it perhaps unexpected. It is the loose ends, the stuff we neither expect nor can explain, that pushes us toward theoretical breakthroughs" (p. 176).

Here are three examples of anomalies from the present study—cases that one might analyze to see how and why they go against general trends.

We found that most therapists tended to restrict their discussion of alternative treatment approaches when talking to clients. This stood out most in the domain of eating disorders which has the widest range of specific treatments of the three areas we looked at. Therapists sometimes avoided talking about alternatives at all and sometimes discussed only the techniques they themselves were prepared to offer. They had various worries about overloading clients with too much information, especially early in therapy. Some were concerned that clients would lose confidence in them and their preferred treatment or that, if a referral was mentioned, the client might feel confused and rejected.

The anomalous case: A therapist who was so eager to thrust treatment options upon her clients, even ones she did not know about herself, that it amounted to a sort of therapeutic anarchy. She had a long list of popular books, including self-help books and autobiographies of people with eating disorders, that she freely distributed to her clients. She urged them to go to the library and search out books, either from her list or by browsing the shelves. This extreme version of what the therapist called the "psychoeducational approach" sometimes backfired.

> Somebody read one I wasn't familiar with. . . . It was one that nobody ever
> chose, anyway. But she managed to find this book . . . in the library. I didn't
> know what she was talking about. I remember saying at the time, did she
> have a copy of it? Did she have it with her? Because I'd like to go through it
> and read it. I think she didn't come back. (T^2)

Such an extreme case gives us a glimpse of what a completely open approach might be like and what its advantages and disadvantages might be.

In our interviews concerning survivors of sexual abuse and sex offenders, we found that therapists generally have a strong ethical stance that confidentiality must sometimes be broken to protect the public. Thus, if an offender tells a therapist or a treatment group about previously undisclosed abuse, or even current abuse, most therapists insist that the disclosure also be made to police. If the client is unwilling, the therapist breaks confidentiality.

The anomalous case: We interviewed the leader of a group of male survivors who had been abused while serving time in youth institutions. From time to time, one of the survivors would admit in the group that he was abusing underage boys. But the leader, who was himself a survivor, told us he would not under any circumstances break the confidentiality of the group.

> I don't say anything because I am not in a position to judge anyone. I am
> not a police officer. These sessions are very private, and we let the person
> know that we are behind them but what they have done is wrong and,
> morally, you know, it is wrong to do anything like that. But we let them
> judge themselves. (C^{84})

The difference between this case and the near unanimity among other therapists about breaking confidentiality in unusual circumstances provided an opportunity to explore the differences among the therapists. The group leader had some training but was not a professional and did not feel bound by a professional code of ethics. He and other group members had been abused not only within the justice system but *by* the justice system, which was reluctant to take their complaints seriously. Thus, he had great skepticism about the value of reporting to authorities. Finding a case in which the helper puts confidentiality first gave us an opportunity to inquire into the feelings of someone who knows that abuse is taking place, perhaps the same sort of abuse he suffered, but does nothing about it.

The third example comes from chapter 6, which is devoted to treatment of sex offenders. We found that therapists tended to be somewhat skeptical about the link between an offender's crimes and the possibility that he himself had been abused. Some told us there was no connection. Some pointed out that only a minority of sex offenders have been abused. Some said offenders seize on this explanation as an excuse. And some believed that, whether or not the offenders were also victims, treatment had to focus on their own abusive behavior.

The anomalous case: A psychologist well known for his empathic and apparently effective work with sex offenders in prison told us flatly that he believed all of them had been victims of abuse. Those who denied it, he said had probably forgotten. He based his treatment on the notion that offenders, even (or especially) sexual predators, are ritually acting out what happened to them in the past:

> A lot of people will say, "Well, how come somebody who's been abused and would know what it was like can go and do that to another person?" But there's a numbness there to what's really happening. So what we try to do is use techniques that connect them to themselves—their own abuse. If that is successful, that's the best form of empathy training that you can do. All of a sudden he's now feeling his own pain and responding—maybe to something he felt as a kid. It's been blocked out, but now he's beginning to feel and experience it. If that happens, he begins to appreciate what's happened and there's a genuine depth of remorse. (T[43])

This unusual case prompted further questions about the reasons behind the psychologist's views, including the impact of his own history—which he readily shared with us (see chapter 6).

The focus on negative cases in qualitative inquiry helps specify limiting conditions of level-three generalizations and abstractions.

Different Methods for Different Questions

Some researchers see qualitative analysis as either an alternative way of testing formal hypotheses or a picturesque addendum to quantitative methods. I believe, on the contrary, that qualitative analysis is best suited to an entirely different type of inquiry from hypothesis testing. Fine (1996) has observed that different methods produce different data. I would add that different sorts of methods are designed to answer different sorts of questions.

Kidder and Fine (1987) distinguish between two sorts of qualitative research, which they dub *big Q* and *small Q*. "The *big Q* refers to unstructured research, inductive work, hypothesis generation" (p. 59). What they call *small Q* research consists of open-ended questions embedded in hypothesis-testing research. Using their terms, the study presented in this book is an example of *big Q* research.

Another way of framing the difference is to say that qualitative research belongs to the interpretive rather than to the experimental sciences. "Experimental sciences search for laws, interpretive sciences search for meaning" (Geertz, 1973, p. 38).

The purpose of qualitative research is not to make statements about incidence (how many cases occur in a population) or about prevalence (how many people are affected by something). Few qualitative researchers, who often use samples of convenience to collect their data, would think of making claims about prevalence or incidence. Such matters enter qualitative research in a different way. Participants often have their *own* views about incidence and prevalence, and these may guide their actions. In the present research, for instance, therapists expressed their opinions on how usual it is that early sexual abuse is related to later problems such as eating disorders or sexual offending. Such ideas about what is usually the case can shape the therapist's approach to treatment.

Qualitative research is not particularly useful for making group comparisons, such as contrasting treatment methods of psychiatrists versus psychologists versus social workers. The work is simply too intensive to permit the sort of sampling that would address a question like that. Instead of comparing discrete groups, the qualitative researcher tries to include a wide range of examples to show the richness of the phenomenon under study. When Terkel interviewed policemen, prostitutes, and taxi drivers for his book *Working*, he was not comparing these groups to test any hypothesis about how they differ. He was creating a mosaic to give the reader a sense of night work in the city from multiple perspectives.

A scholarly discussion of different research paradigms and the questions and methods appropriate to each can be found in Guba and Lincoln's essay, "Competing Paradigms in Qualitative Research" (1994). They show various ways in which the qualitative approach is a fundamentally different enterprise from hypothesis-testing research. I will not try to repeat their excellent analysis here. Instead, I focus on the starting points of qualitative research with some brief examples drawn from studies mentioned in the introduction and from the present study.

The hypothesis-testing researcher has a very different starting point from someone engaging in qualitative inquiry. The former begins with a theory, works out the implications of that theory and frames them as testable hypotheses, and then collects data and usually submits it to quantitative analysis. The sorts of questions that spur qualitative inquiry have a different feel.

Garbarino and Bedard began their study of serious crime by adolescents with the general proposition that there is no such thing as senseless violence. This goes against common accounts that refer to youth crimes as "senseless." By starting from the opposite position, they undertook to see if they could make sense of what *seems* senseless (Garbarino, 1997).

Way (1998) began by asking how it feels to be a teenager in an American city at the close of the twentieth century. What does child development look like when it is framed in the lives of urban teenagers and understood through their own accounts of everyday experience, with all its risks and aspirations? She was interested, too, in how these youngsters' perceptions of themselves are affected by the negative media images that daily bombard them.

Marecek and Kravetz (1998) wondered what range of ideas is embraced by feminist therapy. As they interviewed therapists who called what they did feminist therapy, they tried to find common themes that would link apparently disparate approaches. As the common core became more elusive, they posed the further question, Is it realistic to impose a uniform standard on such a loosely defined treatment approach?

Westcott (1988, 1992, 1994) wanted to know what the experience of freedom felt like to different people in different circumstances. He ventured into the middle ground between "sweeping philosophical abstractions and the individual activity of a single person" (1992, p. 85). His interviews explored the variety of practices that people say enhance the feeling of being free, and he tried to find conceptual links between those practices and philosophical and abstract conceptions of human freedom.

In the present study, I began with a reasonable amount of information about legal and ethical pressures on health professionals to obtain informed consent from their clients (this background was presented in chapter 1). Then I wondered how these consent pressures might play out in psychotherapy, which evolves over time. I was interested in whether psychotherapists took seriously the increasing pressure to tell clients about alternatives and, if so, what alternatives they considered and when they thought the clients should know about them. Finally, when I knew that we would be able to interview some present and former psychotherapy clients, I wondered what *their* experience of consent practices had been: were they satisfied, or would they have preferred to have more information—and what sort of information?

Rather than starting with a hypothesis to be falsified, the big-Q researcher may start with some loosely theoretical questions, including the sorts of "what if" questions that emerge from case to case or interview to interview. If the "what if" questions arise in time, they are posed directly to participants; if they arise later, they are asked of the data as analysis proceeds. The focus is always on how participants understand their situation, as we try to make sense of the sense they make of their world.

4

■ ■ ■ ■ ■ ■ ■ ■ ■

Clients with Eating Disorders

THIS CHAPTER focuses on therapy with clients who suffer from eating disorders—primarily anorexia or bulimia. Interview material from therapists and clients concerns the negotiating process in therapy, the presentation and control of treatment options, and the discussion between therapist and client of underlying factors in the disorder.

To provide a context for how therapists handle these issues, I have chosen to start with a sketch of two clients and their experience of various therapeutic approaches. These clients, whom I call Marie and Deborah, both suffered from eating disorders but were also victims of sexual abuse when they were children. This combination is not unusual. Some therapists believe that there is a causal relation between a history of abuse and later development of an eating disorder, at least in some cases. This view provides one of the underlying factors that might be discussed in therapy.

Other therapists believe that there are very different dynamics at work for eating disordered patients who have suffered child abuse and for those who have no such history. If so, the presence or absence of abuse might call for different treatment approaches, and this is another matter for potential discussion. Those clients, like Marie and Deborah, who are survivors of sexual abuse and who also suffer an eating disorder face a question of which problem should be addressed in therapy, or which should be addressed first.

All these issues are potential matters for negotiation between therapist and client, although, as we will see, therapists differ greatly in whether they negotiate, how they negotiate, and what issues they feel are appropriate or inappropriate to negotiate.

Let's begin, then, with a look at two clients and their voyage through the health system. It was a voyage that would take them, eventually, to the same therapist. At the time of our interviews, both were satisfied with their relationship with their therapist, but they had been disillusioned by previous encounters with health professionals.

Marie was forty at the time of the interview. She had battled bulimia, anorexia, and depression since she was twenty. The eating disorder started later for her than for most clients. She gained weight after having a child and thought of bulimia as a way to control it. Later she turned to binging and purging whenever she felt under stress.

> I grew up in a very dysfunctional family with an alcoholic father who used to try to sexually abuse me. He never [succeeded], but he used to try, and that was trauma enough for me. When I was around sixteen or seventeen, I just didn't think I could live at home any more because it was just hell 'cause he was drunk like all the time. It was just—I didn't think that I could survive. He used to say, "You can't do anything until you're twenty-one." Well, it wasn't twenty-one, but I didn't know that. So I thought well if I end up getting pregnant and get married, I'll live happily ever after and then I'll be away from my family, but it didn't work that way at all. (C[41])

Over the next twenty years she had various unsatisfactory encounters with the health system. Marie described her interaction with a dietitian who tried to deal with her anorexia:

> It didn't help because I felt that she wanted me to eat so much and I just couldn't deal with that.I told her it was too much and she'd drop it down a bit, but really it was a lot, eating something like seven to eight vegetables and fruits a day and five to six cereals and breads. I'd be really fat if I ate all that. I wanted her to put me on a diet of about twelve hundred calories so that at least I was just taking in that. But she didn't do that. She said, "Make eating really automatic. Just go ahead and do it." But it's not that simple. You just can't "go ahead and do it." If I do, I'm really depressed.

And as I eat I can feel the weight coming on me. I feel the fat laying on my legs, my hips. I can really feel it even though it's probably not happening. (C^{41})

If there was little negotiating with the dietitian, there was even less when she saw medical doctors, including psychiatrists.

I'd seen psychiatrists and doctors off and on, but mostly they just give you antidepressants, tranquilizers, sleeping pills. And then I was an addict for prescription tranquilizers and sedatives. The psychiatrist I was seeing was the one that started me on all the pills, and it just got to a point where I had to go and tell him that I wouldn't see him any more. I wouldn't take any more of his drugs. He had me on like fifteen different pills. He knew I was abusing them, but he still gave them to me. (C^{41})

Marie never felt she had any options in therapy until she met her current therapist. Before that, she believed that she was simply being treated according to whatever approach the therapist tended to use with most clients.

Deborah was a twenty-year-old who, unlike Marie, developed an eating disorder very early—at about seven or eight years old. A horrendous history of sexual abuse within her family began even earlier.

It started when I was three with my father, and it continued until I was fifteen, the year before I left home. But it wasn't just him. It was a cousin who lived with us . . . there were about thirty people. But my father and Junior, who is the cousin, they were the serious ones.

There was a lot of physical violence and emotional abuse that, of course, always goes along. My mother was physically abusive, and she knew what was going on and she was no support. She wasn't a help at all. So, myself and my younger brother—I have a sister as well but she seems not to have been [abused] at least she's still denying, so I don't know.

My little brother is a drug addict, too. He's also in denial unless I press him, which I don't.

It went on until the year before I left home, when I threatened to blow off the head of whoever came near me—which is probably what I would have done. (C^{47})

Deborah had a child by her own father. She made eleven suicide attempts between the ages of ten and twenty. Still, her eating disorder was almost the sole focus of her previous treatments, and at one point she even had her stomach stapled.

At the time we met her, Deborah was in a lesbian relationship with a nurse who also had an eating disorder. She thought there were good and bad sides to a romantic relationship with someone who has a similar problem.

> My partner is anorexic, and that doesn't help. We sort of feed off each other. She's a psychiatric nurse, and I met her when I was in hospital. I didn't realize at the time that she was anorexic. She's been hospitalized since, too. We're really good and really bad for each other. I'm so busy trying to keep her stable and she's so busy trying to keep me stable we never have to deal with our own junk.
>
> It's really convenient having another person who has really serious problems 'cause you can just focus on the other person. "Do as I say, not as I do" type of thing. We really support each other, and we relate. Our relationship is very therapeutic. (C[47])

Both Marie and Deborah were diagnosed borderline personality by psychiatrists who, in both cases, told the clients the diagnosis. Both felt that the diagnosis was supposed to "explain" their eating disorder. Their discouraged reaction bears out an observation by Suzanne Kirschner (1997), who maintains that handing a diagnostic label to clients is giving them a warning not to expect very much from psychotherapy.

Marie remembers:

> The doctor that saw me when I was in the hospital really thinks I'm borderline personality disorder. After my breakdown he said that I never could work again—that working just puts too much stress on my life. So that's kind of scary, you know, 'cause there's been points where I thought I would like to work, but I don't think I could work full time because I get depressed at times. (C[41])

Deborah was diagnosed borderline personality disorder when she was seen as a child, before the age when such a diagnosis ought to be made, according to standard practice. The doctor who made the diagnosis did not know that the client had been the victim of child sexual abuse and, according to Deborah, did not recognize symptoms of dissociation associated with the trauma of sexual abuse.

I know I used to feel really strange like I wasn't in control of my body or I would say things that just were out of character or inappropriate. But I thought it was me. I always thought I was nuts anyway. I did. I thought I was crazy. Now I realize I'm not. I was diagnosed Borderline Personality. I probably spent an hour in his [the psychiatrist's] office playing—he had one of those clicking ball things and that's what I played with. He sat and smoked a pipe and I played with this clicking ball thing and then I'm a borderline personality! We didn't talk about anything. I was a little kid—probably fourteen. And how they can make a diagnosis like that? That's something I really want to confront, and sometime soon. It upsets me now 'cause something could have been done at that point and nothing was. (C[47])

Deborah told us that even though she was only twenty, she did not expect a solution to her eating disorder, which she linked to her history of abuse.

This is going to be a lifelong struggle apparently. It may not be this serious for the rest of my life, as I get a handle on other things. I've sort of resigned myself to the fact that I'm gonna fight with this body until the day that I die. It was the only thing I had control over. You're gonna hear every sexual abuse victim say the same thing. The weight, the food that they ate, was the only thing that they had any control over. And that's true. I'm no different than anybody else in that way. (C[47])

Marie and Deborah both wanted to work with a female therapist, partly because their histories of sexual abuse made it difficult for them to trust a male therapist. Nevertheless, they were rarely given a choice in the matter. Marie said that expressing a preference seemed to guarantee she would be given the contrary.

Some of them thought that just on the basis that I didn't want a male that I should have a male. I've always felt like they were saying they were in charge; "the person [potential therapist] is there to help you." I never really had enough courage to go against them. (C[41])

Both of these clients eventually found a therapist in whom they had confidence. Marie said at first she merely wanted to switch to a woman therapist. She said, "I finally got her. She's probably made the most difference in my life so far." Let's turn now to the interactions between clients and therapists that seem to make that sort of difference.

Negotiating Consent

I begin with Marie and Deborah's current therapist, then move on to the negotiating styles of other therapists. They come from a variety of disciplines, including psychiatry, psychology, and social work. The therapist who was seeing Marie and Deborah was a woman in her thirties who had a master's degree in nursing. She identified herself as a community mental health worker, and her practice was in a rural area. At the time of the interview, she had been seeing clients with eating disorders for five years. She also had clients who were survivors of sexual abuse and some, like Marie and Deborah, who were in both categories.

Her preferred approach was gestalt therapy, developed by Perls (1969). But although she liked gestalt techniques (the "empty chair" and so on), her main emphasis was on developing an empathic relationship with clients. Without that relationship therapy would not work; within that relationship she was willing to try a variety of techniques.

> I negotiate. I hear their story and then I interpret it back to them from how I've heard it. Then I ask them what they expect or what they want from therapy—what their goals are. Then I exchange with them or tell them what I think; how I would work with them, with their problem.
>
> Even when they agree, and most do, nothing is carved in stone. I don't know if it's going to work either. I don't know how it fits with their way of thinking or their lifestyle or whatever. And if it doesn't work, well, these are all just techniques. The main thing is understanding the problem and finding a technique that works with them, that fits their personality or their situation. And so sometimes it's trial and error.
>
> The [important] thing is knowing that they're not a failure if it doesn't work. You can suggest something and if it doesn't work, we'll try something else. Doesn't mean that they've failed. It just means it may not fit with their personality. And so then we try something else. It takes off the pressure and often probably it enhances the chances of something even working. (T[25])

She discussed underlying factors with clients, but not in the context of a formal diagnoses. She had not labeled either Marie or Deborah as borderline personalities, even though they had been so labeled by others. People with eating disorders, in her view, tended to be overdiagnosed—usually with a personality disorder. In her view there was no clear relationship between an eating disorder and a personality disorder, and one should not be too quick to make such a diagnosis. "I'm very hesitant to label. There you get my bias—some people are much quicker to organize symptoms into diagnoses."

Both Marie and Deborah liked the fact that their therapist did not deal with them in terms of diagnostic labels. Deborah told us:

> She's the first person that said, "I believe you," and for that reason she's always gonna be really close to my heart. She's the only one who was able to get through layers and layers of defensiveness—this huge wall I had built. She's worked just as hard as I have. She's the first person who told me I wasn't crazy. (C[47])

Sharing with clients a view of etiology does not require consideration of a formal diagnosis. Rather, negotiation involves the fit between the client's perception of personal life events and the meanings attached to them and the therapist's training and experience with other clients.

In relation to underlying factors, this therapist did not make any quick assumption that a client who presented symptoms of an eating disorder was probably a victim of childhood sexual abuse. She had patients with anorexia and bulimia for whom a history of sexual abuse seemed to play a role, and others where there was no such link.

She was one of those therapists who believe eating disorders represent different dynamics for the sexual abuse survivor and for someone without that history. Her experience had led her to a working hypothesis about two sorts of dynamics for eating disorders in adolescents and young adults. One was connected with sexual abuse, and the underlying dynamic was loss of self-esteem as a result of the early trauma. She said, "Weight is a source of protection for them, hiding the slim girl that was sexually abused." In the second scenario, where abuse played no part, the dynamic had to do with a battle for control. She found the abused clients were more open to discussion of underlying dynamics than were clients with similar eating problems but no history of abuse. She said that children from abusive backgrounds knew that something was wrong in their families and understood that childhood trauma would have negative impact on self-esteem. The nonabused clients are often high achievers from families in which there is great pressure to live up to high expectations. "Everybody is expected to achieve and it's supposed to be the ideal typical family, right? She doesn't want to give that up."

Negotiation between therapist and client does not guarantee smooth sailing. The two may discover, for example, that they have fundamentally different ideas about causal factors. Later in this chapter we will see the problems that arise when therapists root eating disorders in the family system while their clients are convinced that cultural factors such as the thin-is-beautiful stereotype are the real problem.

Even when there are no such serious disagreements, clients who have developed strong skepticism about health professionals may find it difficult to trust any therapist. Deborah described the ups and downs of her relationship with her current therapist.

> A lot of it was building trust; I didn't trust anybody. I can probably count on one hand the people that I trust now. That's probably not going to change. It takes forever to gain my trust. Most people just give up and say, "That's it. It's just not worth it." It took us a long, long time; in the end it was worth it.
>
> We have our high points and our low points. Some days I just stomp out of there and say I'm never coming back just because she's making me do exercises that I think are futile. Sometimes I feel like a guinea pig 'cause she's trying out all these new [techniques], but we evolve.
>
> It was touch and go. We learned as we went along. I had no boundaries. When I went in, I was game for anything. I say that, but I was game for nothing. I had no sense of propriety or appropriateness. We went through months and months and months of just discussing boundaries and what was right and what was not right and what I could expect and what I couldn't expect and what her boundaries were. (C[47])

Many other examples of negotiation with clients came out of our interviews; I turn now to some of these variations. It is important to emphasize that we did not find any strong link between negotiating style and profession, gender, or work setting. The next therapist I discuss, for example, was a male psychologist who worked in a university counseling center and whose revolving clientele did not fit the sort of long-term approach that Marie and Deborah's therapist was free to take. He had a strong respect for his college student clients and believed they had the capacity to engage in a dialogue about their problems and treatment options. He, too, found that clients who came for help with one problem might have other potential issues that could be dealt with in therapy. But he was willing to treat the problem as the client defined it.

These are competent people. I'm up front about it. I'll say, "I know this is all you want to do, but here's what I think." But then basically you leave it up to them. If they say, "I just wanted to focus on changing this particular type of behavior"—it doesn't hurt people to work on reducing their bingeing. So even though I think that it's not all we can do, or even the most beneficial thing we can do, in the final analysis I still believe it's beneficial. Let's just work on that; we'll just limit to that and we'll see how it goes. I think that it may not be sufficient, but I'm willing to give it a try and I tell them, "Look, if it works out well, and it's fine for you, and you just eliminate that behavior and that's all you want to do, that's fine." (T^9)

Negotiation does not require that clients have the intellectual capacity of college students. One of our respondents was a male psychologist in a psychiatric day hospital that mandated only short-term therapy with its outpatient population. He worked with compulsive overeaters as well as with anorexics and bulimics. Even within the constraints of brief psychotherapy, he found it important to maintain a constant interchange with clients about his emerging view of them and their problems.

What I have to do at the beginning of the interview is to try to give them a sense as to the sorts of things that I consider to be factors which have affected their ability to make changes in their eating patterns.

Some of them aren't quite sure as to whether they really want this. Part of what I'm trying to do is help the two of us make a decision as to whether we're going to get past this or not. I give them feedback on how I see things, this is what I would recommend. And we hash out, does this make sense to you, do you understand why I'm suggesting this? There's usually a variety of things, and we negotiate a bit and we decide what makes sense. Some people do stop at that point.

When I'm seeing people, I'm trying to develop a model of the person's life in terms of where eating fits in. I'll develop something on paper for the patient as part of the feedback process in the second interview. As I go through this assessment procedure with people and give them feedback, I am trying to get them to look at having different sorts of goals. Now, sometimes over the course of treatment, let's say we're doing some behavioral stuff and things aren't going well. Then, people may say, well, this isn't working. But, more often it actually leads into a really good discussion about how they tend to beat themselves up. How they set themselves up for failure and for being mad at themselves. And so then we start some really productive work on these sorts of issues. (T^{10})

When discussing the history of Marie and Deborah, I cited their dissatisfaction with the psychiatrists they saw. It is important not to give the impression that all psychiatrists act this way, or fail to negotiate with their clients about treatment options or underlying processes. Our next therapist, for instance, is a woman psychiatrist who works with children and adolescents. In the older age group, she often deals with eating disorders. Even with a population under the legal age of consent, this psychiatrist believes it is important to come to an understanding with her clients about what she thinks they need and what she thinks she can do.

> I try to do as full an assessment as I can and come to some understanding in my own mind and with the patient of what I think the issues are. Now, the issues that I see may not be the issues the patient sees.
>
> I am driven by what I think is the most economical approach to a problem—economical to the patient, because it's a busy world and I can't be there to mother everybody. So I will then say to the patient, "Look, to get through this, these are the factors that I think are very important. How do you feel about that? You and I may agree or disagree, but if we agree, this is what I may have to offer you. This is the way I think we should go about it."
>
> I think you have to make clear your goals; you have to determine the fit between what the adolescent thinks the change should be and what you think the change should be. And they can be quite different.
>
> There are some patients with whom to come to that decision takes a number of sessions—even to find out what really is going on. The eating disorder may not turn out to be the central problem. (T[4])

In our sample of clients and former clients, most were strongly in favor of an open negotiation between therapist and client. The following former client, a woman in her twenties, made an argument for early negotiation. First, she described how her therapy ended:

> This therapist seemed to have just read *Psychology Today;* she would spew out things about "toxic parents" and all sorts of these catch phrases, and I just stopped seeing her. She phoned me up and said, "I'd like to know why you've stopped coming." I couldn't tell her that I didn't think she was particularly competent. (C[11])

In the view of this young woman, a poor relationship with one therapist may put the client off therapy altogether. Without having options explained, the client does not understand that this was just one form of therapy and that there are other modes of helping.

> My reaction when it wasn't working with this one therapist was to leave and just never call again. Whereas [it would be different] if you know from the outset that you've got other options. If somebody is saying very clearly, "I approach things from a specific perspective. If you want, we can really give this a try. But I want you to know that, that if you don't like this, there are other opportunities, other options that you can follow." I think it might be better to lay that out at the beginning than to wait until it doesn't work. Because I think you might lose somebody before you can get around to telling them that there's something else. And they may not go back, they may not try and find something else. Because if you haven't let them know that there's something else, they may just think that that's what therapy is. (C[11])

Some therapists believe that eating disorders involve a battle for control, both within the family and later in treatment. For that reason, they are reluctant to be drawn into any negotiation at all. The problem was expressed to us by a psychologist who was a team member of an inpatient group program that enjoyed a good reputation among referral sources.

> You have to consider that one psychological struggle of people with eating disorders is that they are attempting to control something that's ultimately outside of our control. We can lose weight or gain weight, but our body does have a certain course that it will take and you're fooling yourself if you think that you can exert too much control over that. It's our experience that it rarely is helpful to argue that issue, because ultimately if the control is that important to the person, they're not going to take the responsibility that they need to take to work on overcoming the disorder. (T[7])

We found clients disliked the authoritarian style in which there is no negotiation about treatment objectives. They often felt that therapists were condescending to them. This opinion was expressed by a thirty-year-old single mother who had returned to university after parting from her alcoholic, manic-depressive husband.

> I really don't like being treated like I don't know anything and the person behind the desk does. I don't like to spend any time in the doctor's office. There is sort of "I know everything there is to know, and you have come to me for my wisdom." And I am thinking, "Wow, wait a minute. It is my life.

It is my body and I know what is going on in here better than you do. You're somebody whose skills I may need to fix what I know is wrong." You know, I don't like this thing of me being a piece of meat and you are trying to figure out what is the matter with the meat. I have no tolerance or patience for that at all. (C^{54})

The same client had another bad experience with a rational-emotive therapist, a woman working at a free clinic:

I was sent to this woman who is said to be an expert in this area, and it was just horrible from beginning to end. I didn't go very long. I recognize it now as being one of these reality-based types: rational-emotive—very "in your face" and that just did not work with me. I didn't like it that she would basically insult me: "You're self-centered. You're just doing this for attention." It's insulting—those were offensive things to say to me. There is nothing about it that I found even remotely useful, and in fact it made me more depressed, and more anxious, and I ate more, and purged more, and I began exercising like three and four hours a day—it was just wild. It was definitely damaging because things got a lot worse after that. (C^{54})

In our interviews, we were not comparing professions or orientations. We expected to find successful and unsuccessful therapists across these formal categories, and we did. A person with an eating disorder often sees an array of health professionals. The next client was a university student, living at home, who had begun experimenting with bulimic strategies when she was in junior high school and had bulimic periods from then on. She had received treatment from a psychiatrist and a dietitian, neither of whom she liked because they seemed authoritarian. First, her account of the dietitian:

She just basically said, "Stop doing this right now. You're killing yourself, don't do this and do this and this and this—here's the Food Guide—blah blah blah."

My whole purpose was, "Okay, I'm going to go see someone that's going to help me lose weight." And her whole purpose for me being there was, "Let's fill you full of all these good foods." All I wanted was some sure-fire, quick, easy route to losing weight. There was never, "Can we talk about it?"

From the first day I went to her, she was really condescending. She was patronizing. It was like she wanted a case she could just take under her wing and solve the whole bulimic thing and get credit for it. She wanted me to eat so much. For me it was just an overwhelming amount, after eating a soda cracker and feeling guilty. She wanted me to eat, and I wanted to lose weight. I told her that from the beginning, and she just ignored it. For her to say, "Eat this melon salad here, and eat this grilled fish cake here"—I mean, kids don't eat stuff like that. So it was very hard for me to absorb all that information into my lifestyle where I'm having hash browns and pizza all the time and stuff like that. I detested her. I stopped going. (C[32])

When she threatened to take her life, she was referred to a psychiatrist. His approach was different from the dietitian's. He was interested in linking current symptoms to family relationships. But this tack did not suit the client's view of the problem, either.

I was there because I was suicidal. He went back to the bulimia, and then he went back to my relationship with my dad. But it was a separate issue. I'm sure part of my depression was, "I don't like my body and myself"; but they just were so separate. My mother was in the room with me; when we got out of there she said, "I can't believe that guy."

He wouldn't let me talk. I would try and interrupt him, to get that little word in edgewise and contradict him or something, and he would just, "Nah, nah, nah—just wait; I'll give you a chance to talk at the end." It was the funniest thing, so I just sort of sat there and listened to him preach at me. When we came out we started to laugh about it. (C[32])

This client told us that the best helping relationship she had ever experienced was with her high school guidance counselor.

She's definitely the most successful one that intervened with me. She was very approachable, and she never tried to get at the roots of the problem, like, "Oh this is going back to a lousy childhood" or any of this type of stuff. Which a lot of people did afterwards. It was it was more like, "Well, what do you have to say?", and she let me talk and tell her what I had to say. She never was like, "Oh we've got to get you to a doctor right away." She was like, "Well, I'm a little concerned you know, I think this might be a good idea. Can I run this by you?" She let me make my own decisions about everything.

I think therapy has to be more two-sided like my relationship with her. The other sessions I went to [with other health professionals] weren't really therapy. They weren't, "I'm going to discuss my problem with you and try and find some solutions or try and find some other roads that we can take."

> The other people I saw were just, "Sit down and let's talk about the bu-
> limia, or the problem with your dad," or whatever. And it was just, "Let's
> pinpoint it and get out of here." I think when you just sit down and talk
> about all types of issues, a lot more comes out. A lot more information is vol-
> unteered and a lot more things are discovered and are examined. (C^{32})

These are some perspectives on the general process of negotiation in the relationship between a therapist and a client with an eating disorder. I move now to the question of presenting alternative treatment possibilities to clients. I have identified this as an increasing source of pressure on therapists who probably know they must gain full, free, informed consent if they are to meet both ethical and legal requirements.

Presenting Alternatives

Of the three problem areas covered in this book, eating disorders have by far the widest array of specific treatments. Potentially, they also provide the most opportunity (or obligation) for a therapist to discuss alternatives with clients.

Here is a quick, partial survey of the sorts of treatments that various authors have recommended for bulimia and anorexia: Monitor the client's food purchase and eating, to control eating patterns; don't monitor, to avoid reinforcing the client's preoccupation with food. Give the client a daily exercise program with weight chart, to show other means of weight control besides starving or purging; don't initiate an exercise program, to avoid reinforcing the client's over-concern with body image. Teach patients about nutrition and balanced approach to eating; resist the client's obsessive discussions about food and try to turn the client toward deeper issues such as feelings of loneliness.

There is more: Give cognitive-behavioral therapy to control maladaptive eating patterns; use progressive relaxation training to reduce tension; emphasize insight-oriented therapy to deal with underlying emotions; provide supportive (relationship) therapy to help the client fill an emotional void; treat relationship issues from a psychoanalytic perspective, working through transference.

A range of physical therapies have also been proposed. These include biofeedback for control of autonomic functions (the client "feels full" when taking very little food). Medications have been recommended to deal with a variety of symptoms or related problems—medications to reduce anxiety, to kick-start the appetite, to lower depression, to decrease obsessive rumination about food and weight.

There is also some debate about whether one should hospitalize a client suffering from an eating disorder. I will not discuss hospitalization in any detail, since it is often used to keep anorexic patients from starving to death. When employed for this reason, it is less a treatment alternative than a life-saving measure to buy time for other treatments to be used. Nevertheless I should note that even in nonemergency situations, some therapists recommend hospitalization to enforce dietary control, while others believe that it draws the client into a power struggle.

The variety of treatments I have surveyed are, of course, based on different ideas about the genesis of eating disorders—what is "really wrong" with an anorexic or bulimic client. For example, the therapist who provides social skills training believes the client has trouble with relationships. The behavior therapist who works to control a maladaptive eating pattern and the dietitian who provides information about nutrition believe the problem is more closely related to the symptom. I will take this matter up later, when considering how therapists discuss with clients their notions about underlying factors.

There are many other treatments, and treatment rationales, besides those I have mentioned here. For a good recent presentation of the range of treatments for bulimia and anorexia, I recommend Garner and Garfinkel's (1997) *Handbook of Treatment for Eating Disorders.* My purpose has been primarily to show that there are many alternatives that can be offered to clients, or at least discussed between therapist and client.

Among the clients we interviewed, most wanted more alternatives than they had been given by therapists, and some were adamant about this, blaming the failure of a therapy experience on the lack of negotiation over type of treatment. A former client pointed out that it is not enough to say that alternatives exist without providing some information about them.

> When I went in, he said, "Well there are a number of different things that we can do," and then he started me off on behavior modification. He never told me what the options were. I think if he had told me, that would have been a lot more useful than saying, "There are different ways that we can go

at this, but let's start with this." I think I would have found it more useful if he had given me some idea of what those other options were, because behavior modification sort of intensified the problem. (C[54])

In the absence of information provided by her therapist, she tried to find it on her own. But she had difficulty sorting through the literature. She was skeptical about articles in the popular press and she did not have the background to understand the reports in scientific journals.

I worked in the library, and any time I could get my hands on stuff, I would read it. At that time, though, all I had access to was scientific journals and articles. I don't read popular magazines—I didn't read any of that stuff at all. And, of course, reading scientific journals was fine if you had any kind of training. Otherwise, the terminology is impossible to wade through. It is just ridiculous. So I wasn't getting a whole lot out of that. (C[54])

Clients do not always take a benign view of the reasons therapists fail to provide information about other treatments, especially options that might involve referring the client to someone else. A former anorexic patient looked back on the issue with some skepticism.

Should a therapist just say, "This is what I offer," instead of saying, "These are the possibilities?" It seems that that really serves the therapist. I think a lot of people going to therapy for the first time would just kind of go, "Oh, okay, this is what you give. All right." Instead of knowing that there are other things. It just seems like that might be a way for therapists to sort of keep clients—rather than mentioning alternatives. (C[11])

There is an increasing consumerist stance among members of the public who find themselves in need of therapy. They are less and less willing to accept the mystique of the health professions and increasingly employ metaphors that equate therapy with commercial exchanges. Here is a former bulimic, comparing therapy to buying clothes:

We know our own selves and we should be able to figure out what is best for us. It's like when you go into a clothing store—you know which clothes you're going to feel comfortable in and what you like. I think it's the same with therapy. (C[18])

Some health professionals are willing to think about their enterprise in similar ways, and even to employ similar metaphors to explain the negotiating process that should take place. In chapter 1 I quoted a psychologist in a university counseling center who compared himself to a garage mechanic, negotiating about car repair. Some therapists are much less sanguine about seeing themselves in consumerist terms. A psychologist working at a psychiatric day hospital used a hairdresser metaphor to indicate the way he did *not* want to be treated by clients.

> There are certain warning signals I get from people in the initial interview, that they want to determine what is going to happen here. And they basically want me to be like a hairdresser. It's not so much that this person wants to have choice in treatment, it's that they want to control what's happening. (T[10])

His distinction between choice and control is an interesting one. He felt that, while clients should be told about options, they should not have control of the therapy process.

One treatment option over which clients were given little choice or control, we found, was whether to have individual or group therapy.

Group versus Individual Treatment

Researchers who study eating disorders have offered a number of reasons to explain why group treatment may be helpful to this population. Clients with anorexia and bulimia generally suffer from interpersonal distrust, low self-esteem, unrealistic ideas about nutrition, and distorted body image. As Polivy and Federoff (1997) point out, the group format provides interpersonal validation, information, enhanced self-esteem, and feelings of control through helping oneself and others.

The mere presence of other members may provide some of the same things whatever the orientation of the therapist (for instance, all groups provide feedback to the client from people with similar problems). Nevertheless, group psychotherapy is not a single entity. There are a variety of group approaches ranging from psychoeducational (short-term treatment and information giving) to psychodynamic (long-term treatment that focuses on the deeper meanings of symptoms). There are also self-help groups in which there is no professional, and thus no professional's orientation. Self-help groups offer interpersonal acceptance and encouragement.

Clients expressed a wide variety of opinion about the value of groups. Among those who thought the group experience was positive, there were two main themes in the explanations. I call the first the *empathic* theme and the second the *comparison* theme. In the first case, a group is seen as helpful because people can empathize with others who have similar problems. In the second case, the value of the group lies in comparing oneself with others who are worse off and deciding not to be like them.

To begin with the empathic theme, here again is the mature student who, at the time we interviewed her, had recently left her abusive, alcoholic spouse. She was in a self-help group for people with eating disorders.

> Being in that group was actually my first time, ever, being in a group of women. I really didn't know how women thought or how they experienced things. I have always hung out with men and with boys, and most of my friends are male. So it was a unique experience to be around women, and it was one that was very rewarding. It made me look at being female differently. It sort of gave me an idea of what it is to be a female because I really wasn't sure. It was all sort of confused. (C[54])

Often a client must be seen individually before a group experience can be productive. At the outset of this chapter I introduced Deborah, a twenty-year-old with a history of child sexual abuse, suicide attempts, and bulimia. Her therapist suggested she go to a group, but she could not handle the experience. Later in her treatment, however, the therapist encouraged the reluctant client to try again, with better results. Again, the empathy theme emerges:

> She suggested that I do this group that she was running and I lasted for probably twenty-five minutes—hyper-ventilating and dissociating. An ambulance ended up coming, and I'm whisked away. So I said then I would never do another group, but [my therapist] asked me as a favor to do this group for these two people that she knew. And she wanted me to try it because she thought it, you know, could be of some benefit, and it was. There's something about being with other women who are of like mind. If you're having a rotten day, it's great not to have to explain. Normal people just don't understand. Some days I'm just really off, and these people didn't need explanations and they understood a lot. (C[47])

The contrast theme emphasizes the confrontational aspect of a group. A bulimic university student told us that only those who have similar problems can really challenge the defensive views of others.

> Being in a room with people that are going through the same thing is good. These people [health professionals] that just study it and don't live it have a tendency to want to preach at you and shove all the literature they've absorbed down your throat. It all comes down to—a person has to feel that they need to go there; a lot of times with bulimia it's like, "I don't need any help." Just like alcoholism, I suppose, "I don't need help, I don't, I'm fine, I can deal with this myself." (C[32])

The connection with alcoholics was also made by another client, who exemplifies the contrast theme regarding the value of groups. This young woman suffered from bulimia in her teen-age years. At the time we interviewed her, she was a graduate student, and she is now a psychologist. She thought that seeing and talking to others with eating disorders forces clients to see how foolish their behavior and preoccupations are. She had been seen individually by a behavior therapist and later, briefly, in a small group run by the same therapist.

> The best session I had with her [the therapist] was when other people came. There were a couple of other girls who were bulimic and anorexic. And that made a difference, because there was one girl there who was anorexic, she was so thin—skinny. The other girl was very healthy looking, but she was bulimic. There were three of us and we used to look at this girl, and I always liked telling her how stupid she was, because she was so thin: "You're too thin, honey, you don't look good." (C[18])

This notion of comparing oneself with others who have a worse version of the same problem was repeated by a number of clients. Here is a dietitian who had suffered from an eating disorder:

> Group helped me because I knew I didn't want to be as bad as everyone else. I didn't want to be like them. I didn't want people to think of me like they thought of them. It's snotty, but it worked. They were messed up. I remember there were quite a few of them that had alcoholic parents and I never did, so like I couldn't contribute to that. (C[19])

Comparison and confrontation are not for everyone. Sometimes groups do not work for some clients precisely because of the tendency to, as they see it, pick on one another. We had this reaction from an adult woman with two children, who was still bulimic at the time we interviewed her:

> I did do a group therapy thing. It just didn't pan out the way it was supposed to, I guess all you do is pick everybody else apart. It's almost like you know who's sicker, and everybody's down on the one that's absolutely the sickest. Everybody wanted to be the skinniest and vomit the most. You could see people rolling their eyes at the one that was absolutely the worst. (C[22])

These, then, are the views of some clients about their experiences in groups. What of the therapists? We found that whether or not they used group therapy depended more on organizational and financial considerations than on any theory about the effectiveness of groups or screening of individual clients. A psychologist in a university counseling center acknowledged that there were clients who could benefit from group treatment, but the center did not use groups for fear of compromising confidentiality.

> We've made some initial inquiries of a number of our clients; when I phrase the question with individual clients, the tendency has been to say, "No, I wouldn't be interested." Partly I think it's because [this university] is such a small community. Girls in recovery consider this an area of privacy. And they just don't want to be identified with a group that could become high profile. (T[3])

If a university setting puts a premium on privacy, such is not the case in large hospitals that draw clients from a wide area. In a program located in one such hospital, we found that group treatment was not only looked on with favor but was virtually the only therapy offered to eating-disordered clients. The program's excellent reputation had led to a stream of referrals and a long waiting list. The psychologist who worked with the program told us that it used groups for economic reasons. There were too many clients needing help and too few therapists to permit the luxury of individual treatment for anyone. He rationalized this severe constraint on treatment choice by explaining that it served as a screening mechanism to determine whether clients were really motivated. If they were, they took the treatment offered. If they were not, they dropped out.

In our clinic we don't give them the alternative of individual or group therapy. Everyone is brought in with the expectation that they will go through our group process. If we gave them the choice, they would always choose individual therapy, because they get concerned or frightened or distressed by the notion of sitting in a room with other people who have eating disorders. They think the others are looking at them, and they compare—"they're probably thinner than I am." For those individuals who are just absolutely terrified about being in a group, and it's very clear to us that they're experiencing some major difficulties with their eating disorder, we would see them individually for a short period of time to prepare them for the group work—because it's too difficult to turn someone away who needs some help.

If we do lose people, it's probably the same percentage of people who drop out after two or three [individual] therapy sessions. So, I think it's a nice screening in that respect. (T⁷)

Despite his optimistic comment about group treatment as a screening device, this therapist was frank about the important factor being financial. And he realized that applying a single approach necessarily disadvantages some clients.

You can't be everything to everyone, and there's always going to be people who do fall through the cracks. We were hesitant when we decided to make a transition to predominately a group-based approach because we thought some individuals just might not be able to tolerate that. [But] we have to restrict things because of our person power. I think it's a clinical reality that there are going to be people who just do fall through the cracks. (T⁷)

Sometimes the rigidity built into group treatment appears to threaten the individual rights of clients. We found, for example, that such programs are not tolerant of dietary preferences such as vegetarianism, which may or may not be related to a dysfunctional preoccupation with food. It may be an individual moral stand or related to a cultural or religion custom. We interviewed a psychiatrist who was the medical director of a day program. He told us the program had been criticized for its stand against vegetarianism and against exercise. Some of the criticism had come from community groups, and the health professionals were worried that they were on the point of losing community support. Nevertheless, the psychiatrist defended the treatment approach.

Probably the two most controversial issues across our whole treatment program are exercise and the issue of vegetarianism. We'll get somebody in who tells us that they are a committed vegetarian—vegetarian long before they had an eating disorder, and damned if they're going to eat meat in the program.

It's a group therapy program, and everybody has to eat the same way because otherwise nobody would eat. So they have to eat off the hospital menu, which means they have to eat meat. Vegetarianism is a normal variant, and sure some people with eating disorders are going to return to a vegetarian lifestyle, but we can't tell ahead of time whether their vegetarianism is related to their eating disorder or related to committed moral choice, and we can't run our treatment program if someone is allowed not to eat meat and someone else has to. Because then nobody would want to eat. That's the kind of delicate balance you run in a group therapy program.

So basically, nobody can be a vegetarian in our intensive treatment program. That's just the way it is. What we say is, "We want you to eat meat while you're in the program and make a decision about your vegetarianism from the perspective of normal eating." Some people say, "Forget it" and go somewhere else. There were a few very vocal people in the community who had a real problem with this stance. (T[20])

Turning to exercise, the psychiatrist explained why some exercise programs are banned or discouraged:

And the second issue is this business of exercise. We ask people not to exercise until their eating is normal, because, again, we can't tell how much of their exercise is purging and how much of it is—whatever. And that's a problem when we get athletes in. I have a high jumper in here right now who desperately wants to start training again to get ready for the next season. We can't tell what portion of her training regimen, at this point, is eating-disorder related and what is training related. So we say, "Well, get your eating under control first and then start to exercise." This really bugs some people. There's a lot of mixed opinion among the staff of the program. The policy is that you support people being physically active, but we try and aim people—no aerobics, no solitary running and that sort of stuff. We encourage people to take a walk with a friend, go for a bike ride with a friend, play some tennis, something that is social.

As this psychiatrist indicated, staff members tended to have different opinions about such rigid rules. We interviewed a woman psychiatrist who worked in a group program where vegetarianism was not tolerated. She clearly had mixed feelings about the limitation on patient's rights, as well as the stereotypical view that any dietary preference expressed by someone with an eating disorder must be a symptom of the disorder.

> There's a pretty strong feeling among people in eating disorder work that people with eating disorders must learn how to eat every kind of food, and that would include meat. At our hospital it is not acceptable to be a vegetarian. I'm the person who's most outside the medical model on that issue. I know that it can be an indication of so-called eating disordered thinking. What I'm concerned about is the symbolic imagery or images associated with eating meat. And plus I think there's a place for people to be vegetarian. (T[26])

The use of group therapy for all patients is not consistent with either the literature on therapy for eating disorders or the variety of feelings expressed to us by clients. Studies of treatment effectiveness indicate that some clients are better candidates than others for group programs. Patients with low motivation for change may not drop out, as speculated by the psychologist who talking about screening. Instead, they may remain in a group and be extremely disruptive. Although groups improve social skills, people who are too frightened to speak in a group will not gain much from the experience.

There are other reasons that some clients are not well suited to group treatment. Some have other serious problems besides the one around which the group is organized. This was the case with the client Deborah, who had a number of problems including unresolved trauma from serious sexual abuse throughout her childhood. I have quoted her first experience of group therapy: "I lasted for probably twenty-five minutes—hyperventilating and dissociating. An ambulance ended up coming, and I'm whisked away." Polivy and Federoff summarize the literature on suitability for group therapy: "Careful patient assessment and screening are recommended" (1997, p. 470). They say that good screening prepares clients for the group experience and reduces the dropout rate. They are talking about screening *for* group treatment, of course, not using the group to screen out people who are apparently not motivated. These are all strong reasons for thorough client-therapist discussion of group participation as a treatment option.

As with groups, so with other treatments: Different approaches suit different clients. Fairburn (1997) made this point while comparing the use of cognitive-behavioral therapy and interpersonal therapy for people with anorexia or bulimia. He concluded that clients should be matched with type of therapy.

Therapists who we interviewed varied greatly in the amount of information they give to patients in the process of negotiating informed consent. A behavioral psychologist, for instance, liked to pull out the American Psychiatric Association's *Diagnostic and Statistical Manual* and hand it to her clients. She would tell them her tentative diagnosis and invite them to look over symptoms and proposed etiologies and discuss whether the diagnosis fit.

> They want to know as much as possible. I am not above whipping out the diagnostic manual and showing people what I think is wrong with them. The very documents I use to come to a diagnosis I put in their hands and say, "Look, this is what I'm thinking about. Have a look at these symptoms. According to this, if you have six out of these nine symptoms, then you probably have this disorder. Let's go through them and see. What do you think?" People like being part of the process. They like having some input. They like setting you straight when you're wrong. (T[6])

We also interviewed a former bulimic client of this therapist, who was enthusiastic about the therapist's open sharing of such diagnostic information.

> If you pick up a book and you relate to that idea. I think, "Hey, this is me— I can see where she [the therapist] is coming from." And then suddenly everything starts to fall together, and you can start to work from that. (C[18])

Not all therapists would hand their patients texts containing diagnostic criteria. Some would agree with the first therapist I presented in this chapter, who said she was hesitant to label and slow to organize her impressions into a formal diagnosis.

On the other hand, some therapists rely on popular accounts of disorders to acquaint clients with possible etiologies, treatments, and outcomes. We interviewed a mental health nurse whose approach, which she called psychoeducational, was to encourage clients to read popular books, including autobiographies, to learn about anorexia and bulimia. Sometimes she lent books from her own collection; sometimes she sent clients to the library to search for material themselves. The drawback was that she sometimes found herself trying to discuss notions culled from works she had forgotten or had never read.

> We used to provide the patients with a lot of options for reading; we used to keep a library. Somewhere along the line I would give them the list and say to choose just one off the list and read it. A number of them are biographies and autobiographies written by recovered or semirecovered anorexics and bulimics. They would sit and discuss the literature a lot with you. I think they do have to gain information—simple information.
>
> You'd kind of explore it. "What do you think? Do you think that that might relate to you in any way?" If they buy into it, and it makes sense to them, then work with it. (T^2)

This was perhaps the most extreme example of providing options to clients that we came across in all the interviews we did for this book. Many therapists would disagree with it as turning the therapeutic situation into a kind of anarchy. In chapter 3 I quoted this therapist describing the predicament that can arise from this approach. Clients may read books the therapist cannot recall, and their confidence may be undermined.

Not surprisingly, there are therapists who are skeptical about presenting alternatives through popular reading material. A male psychologist in a university counseling center talked about the dangers of relying on the fad of the moment.

> Certainly there are hot topics now. People come in and say, "I've read this. This is me. I want that." There are other hot topics—adult children of sexual abuse and adult children of alcoholics are the ones who are most likely to come in and say, "I've read this book. This is me. I have all those symptoms. I want this treatment." It depends on the group, but some of it could be really simplistic and misleading. So are some of the books that are out. I'm not convinced that people are well served by some of that stuff. (T^9)

The timing of discussion about treatment options is also an issue for psychotherapists. Some told us they were afraid of swamping clients with too much information too soon. The following comments were made by a woman clinical psychologist who held an academic post at a university.

When somebody comes to me with a problem, it's my responsibility to try and help them, if I feel I have something I can offer them. Now, if I feel I cannot offer them anything, then I will recommend this and that. But if they've come to my doorstep, they're not asking for this and that, they're saying, "Can you help me with this problem?"

If the person asked me for information—"What other ways are there to deal with this problem?"—I would tell them. I'm not worried about them knowing. I think it's a choice that they should have.

Basically, I would tell them about these other things if they became unhappy with their treatment. Or if they were not making progress. Or they got better and they were going out and they wanted to know, "What from now on? What for the future? What if this happens again? What can I do?" (T[1])

The interviewer asked whether the client ought not to have the information earlier in therapy, to make an informed choice about mode of treatment. The therapist was skeptical. She made a doctor-patient analogy, using her own asthma as an example.

At the initial step, I don't know. When I go to my doctor and ask for help with my asthma—that's what I've come for. If he was going to point me in every other direction, I would start to wonder whether he was rejecting me. I have this feeling that this is how I would like to be dealt with, too. The doctor can say to me, "Look, I think you need to see a specialist." "You need to go see somebody else." "This is beyond me." I don't know if in therapy we're supposed to do that—when somebody presents with a problem whether we should say, "There are millions of ways we can deal with this problem," and start listing them. (T[1])

This therapist was worried about undermining the client's confidence and risking making the client feel rejected. Presenting alternative treatments (and, by implication, alternative therapists) might suggest that the therapist would rather the client go elsewhere. This worry has been expressed by others who deal with problems that may occur when the therapist is trying to do a thorough job of obtaining informed consent (see, for instance, Hare-Mustin et al., 1995).

Therapists we interviewed saw various problems with running through a list of alternatives in obtaining informed consent. Some of these were practical problems: Although the therapy might be in the treatment literature, it might not be available in the area where the client lived. A psychologist who worked in a university counseling center discussed this problem:

> I don't bother going through treatment approaches that are not available. I mean, I don't get into theoretical discussions with people. I think, this person came to me for help and if they are likely candidates for the treatment I have to offer and that's agreeable to them or it sounds good to them, then I don't get into other possibilities just as a matter of form.
>
> You have to use some judgment in terms of what to focus on. There's always a cost. To go through literally all the possible alternatives would probably take a full session. I don't think that's exaggerating. I don't want to waste their time doing that to cover my agenda.
>
> Some are more vigilant consumers than others. Others will come in amazingly trusting—more than I would be—they just come in and say, basically, "You're the expert, whatever you say."
>
> I consider what the legal system calls a reasonable judgment. Are these likely alternatives that this person might end up pursuing? There are treatments, like gestalt therapy for eating disorders, that would require them to commute to Montreal or California. I never mention that [treatment] to people 'cause in my judgment they are unlikely to do that. So I make that judgment for them.
>
> It's not that I wouldn't trust them to judge—they're competent, they're intelligent. I don't sort of withhold any information because I think they might make the wrong judgment. My concern is about wasting time, talking about things just because we want to play it safe with some code of ethics or something—make sure I cover my ass. And whose agenda is being served? Usually not the client's. (T[9])

Ironically, gestalt therapy for eating disorders *was* available in this therapist's district, although he apparently did not know it—you will recall that the therapist I presented at the outset, who was in the same region as the psychologist just quoted, used gestalt therapy. Perhaps they did not know about each other because they were from different professions (nursing and psychology). Information about specialties tends to be good within professional boundaries but poor across boundaries.

Some therapists consider the written consent form to be essential as a part of the consent process. But even here, there was room for disagreement about the effect that such a form might have on the client's confidence. One young woman, looking back on her experience when she suffered from an eating disorder, said she might be alarmed about the implications of the written form:

> I might worry about actually signing a consent form. I would wonder, what does this mean? It might make me more wary than anything else. I think I would wonder, "Well, if it's *me* who's controlling [therapy], what am I consenting to?" I tend to be suspicious about that kind of thing. You know, when you sign a consent form for gymnastics, that means that if you break a leg, that's your tough luck. I think, "What am I gonna break?" I'd sort of wonder the same thing about the therapy. What are they gonna do that's dangerous? Could they make my problems worse? Or, if I don't like something, maybe I can't do anything about it because I've consented to it. (C[11])

Thus, even the most standard of consent procedures, a written consent form, can undermine confidence or arouse suspicion about what may happen in psychotherapy.

Discussing the Underlying Problem

Many treatments are proposed for clients with eating disorders; they are generally based on different views of the cause of the disorder, either in general or in the specific case. This raises the question of whether it is enough to discuss alternative treatments with clients, unless the therapist is also prepared to talk about etiologies implied by the treatment.

To explore this issue, I focus on one possible underlying factor that many therapists implicate in eating disorders: the relationship between the client and his or her family. We found that therapists are more likely than clients to relate anorexia and bulimia to family problems. Furthermore, views of the role the family plays vary, depending on the therapist's explanatory model. I begin with some of those models.

An early and still popular view of the family is that it operates in ways that produce the eating disorder. The family system is seen as being characterized by dysfunctional roles and alliances, emotional overdependence, and strong tensions that are often not openly or directly expressed. The eating disorder is seen as a symptom of these family dynamics, a relatively safe way for the identified patient to act out anger (Minuchin, Rosman, and Baker, 1978).

Others see the family as a partner in treatment, almost a cotherapist. The family's role with the bulimic patient, for instance, is to set limits: locking the kitchen at night, making the patient pay for all food consumed in binges, denying the patient access to the bathroom for purging and instead making the patient use a special bucket, which the patient must clean (Vanderlinden, Norré, and Vandereycken, 1992).

This "cotherapist" view involves the family directly in controlling food consumption and applying sanctions. But there are others who urge families and therapists not to use punitive methods, which they say damage the patient's self-concept. This line of thinking suggests that punitive methods arise from family anger at the patient, which in turn arises from feelings of helplessness and frustration and anger in caregivers (Goldner, Birmingham, and Smye, 1997).

A recent spin on the problem by Peggy Claude-Pierre of the Montreux Clinic is different from these conceptions. Claude-Pierre (1997) rejects harsh measures toward the patient and denies that eating disorders result from control battles or distorted body image. Instead, she sees patients as having an overly developed moral sense that drives them, in an excess of altruism, to try to shoulder responsibility for everything that threatens the family and all its members. Her prescription is to provide, and to have the family provide, an atmosphere of unconditional love and compassion. Only this, she believes, will cure the patient of pessimism and self-loathing. Claude-Pierre, whose approach is controversial, came to international attention when it was reported that she had been consulted by the late Princess Diana about her bulimia (McInnis, 1997).

Given these starkly different orientations, what might it mean when a therapist says to a client, "I think your family should be involved?" What might the client be agreeing to? Perhaps to family therapy where the focus will be on the dysfunctional system and not on the "symptom"; perhaps to a treatment program in which the family will guard the refrigerator and the bathroom; perhaps to a discussion designed to allay family desperation; or perhaps to a treatment aimed at relieving the patient's responsibility for real and imagined dangers to family members.

All these contradictory approaches to the family have their adherents among therapists. Moreover, many therapists shun the systems approach and link eating disorders to the relationship of the patient to either mother or father. The mother was almost always to blame in the view of one psychologist we interviewed:

> The theme that I hear repeatedly, the one that always comes through, is the control issue between mother and daughter. It's that aspect of being smothered, overcontrolled—there's always the sense of an intrusion by the mother into the space of the adolescent. (T^5)

For that reason, he said, he did not make referrals to female therapists, especially to feminist therapists. Furthermore, he said he had never had a client who asked for such a referral.

> Because, remember, they're the "little girls," and they're desperately seeking some bond with a father image. They're not out to fight the father; they're out to fight the mother. So the feminist therapist becomes the surrogate of the intrusive, aggressive mother. Most of them fit that dynamic. (T^5)

In this example, a male psychologist with a psychoanalytic orientation believed that most females with eating disorders were struggling with their mothers. A female psychologist with a behavioral orientation, on the other hand, insisted that the father was often to blame. Here is the response of one of her clients:

> I felt like saying, "Whether I'm angry with my dad or not, I'm still not happy with my body." I would have loved to blame it on my father. I didn't like my father very much, and if I could make him feel guilty for an eating disorder, then great! But I knew that wasn't the sole reason. And here she was telling me: "Work things out with your father; I think you'll be all right." (C^{18})

Another client we interviewed, a bulimic university student, also referred to her relationship with her father but discounted it as a factor in her eating disorder:

> My father was never, like, "Oh, you need to lose weight" or anything like that. Nor the rest of my family. I don't get along with my father. I mean, we're so separate it isn't funny. But people always want to tie it together, and there's not even a link. (C^{32})

Therapists differ not only in how they place the family in the origin of the disorder but also in their willingness to have the family involved in therapy. The following therapist is typical of those who believe that families are essential to any treatment plan for young clients with eating disorders:

> The family perspective is always my first way in. I ask, "What's going on in the family situation?" because that always seems to be implicated. By involving the family in the therapy process, you're validating to the client that this problem is bigger than them—that it's a very big problem. (T^1)

The interviewer asked how adolescents felt about having their families involved.

> Oh, they are very eager to get to the family. Every time I've dealt with somebody with an eating disorder, they are very eager to get the family involved. Their major complaint is the family will not listen. the family will not see their point of view. (T^1)

Some other therapists believe the family may be part of the cause but is no part of the solution. This is colorfully expressed by a mental health nurse who talked about her experience with parents on an inpatient unit.

> They used to drive us nuts. Families were so intrusive, always hovering like helicopters. They'd kind of perch; they were perchers. The kids needed to be pulled out. But the families would fight that. A lot of stress was put on getting the children established and getting bonds broken. And most of the families didn't like that. We used to have to have some very restricted visiting times for a lot of them. (T^2)

But not all families are eager to be involved in the treatment of a child with an eating disorder. A young woman who was still bulimic when she was interviewed looked back on the failed attempt to involve her family when she was a teenager:

> They brought Mom and Dad in on it. I didn't want to do it. "Well, we think it's best. Do this, do this." So I said, "Fine." So they phoned Mom and Dad to come in. The therapist knew as soon as ten minutes had gone that it wasn't going to work. My parents sat there and said nothing, or "yes", "no", "yes." It just didn't work. They weren't interested at all. Mom and Dad are not that type of people. (C^{22})

If the family had become more involved, this client believed it would have made matters worse. "I know it wouldn't have helped it actually would have made home life miserable."

Family Models versus Social Pressure Explanations

Most therapists we interviewed discounted the role of culture or the media in eating disorders, in favor of a family approach. A male psychologist said that, while culture may play a part,

> I still think that it's some intrapsychic dynamic that established this pattern. These clients are out of balance with their nature and use compensation, forming some type of eating disorder. Somehow these clients have not developed an adequate sense of self-assertion. And so what they typically do is to swallow the garbage of the day. They just seem to be a reservoir of negatives that are said about them or expectations from people who want too much from them. (T[5])

A woman psychologist with a different orientation to therapy nevertheless had similar skepticism about blaming cultural norms:

> If the standard changed in the year 2000, and all of a sudden we were supposed to be a little bit overweight, or women were supposed to be a little bit plump, anorexics wouldn't comply with that. (T[6])

There is, however, one approach—feminist therapy—that gives a significant role to the way in which women are taught to think about themselves by society. Toni Ann Laidlaw coauthor of the feminist therapy text *Healing Voices*, says therapists with this approach "take very seriously the message that [clients] must conform to an image of thinness in order to be valued as women" (1990, p. 17). Many therapists reject the social influence theory because if it were true, more women would be affected. But Laidlaw believes the majority of young women *are* at risk for anorexia and bulimia. She maintains that up to 80 percent of female students on university campuses have borderline to severe eating disorders. In her view, "eating disorders have become the norm for North American women" (p. 17).

The question most relevant to this book is not who is right but whether such matters are discussed between therapist and client. If they are discussed, do therapists and clients tend to have different ideas about the origin of the problem? On the basis of our interviews, we concluded that such a disagreement might well occur.

Young women clients generally told us that they were most interested in whether they were attractive to young men, and that concern, coupled with the thin-is-beautiful stereotype, was more important than any family dynamic. Here is a comment from a bulimic university student:

> When I get really depressed I resort right back to my old habits. What type of things depress me? Guy stuff, thinner girls being around me. If I go to a party like a beach party or pool party and I'm around people that are little thin things I'll be sitting there watching them. Like, how can they be that thin? I need to be like that. Prancing around in bathing suits in front of guys. God, wouldn't that be nice? (C[32])

She talked about the double message that the media present to young women:

> I mean, on the covers of magazines you have a big picture of a cake or something—like, "try this new recipe." And then you have ten ways to be thinner. Such confusing messages that we're being sent. I used to think I would love to go to a society where large women are regarded highly; the cherub age. I used to look at cats and dogs—the fatter they are, the cuter they are. And babies, they're so chubby, they're so cute. We have to be so thin to be beautiful. I just used to wish it was the other way, where the bigger you are the more beautiful you are. So all these scrawny people are ugly. (C[32])

Another university student with an eating disorder related her low self-esteem, which she felt to be central to the problem, to media influences.

> I can look at magazines and think, "Oh, like I want to look like her." I just always want to look like everybody around me, and it probably has an impact. I'd look at clothes on models and think, "Oh, how come that doesn't look like that on me?" but I just think, "Oh that's my fault, I just have to lose weight." (C[21])

A young woman who overcame adolescent bulimia and eventually became a psychologist linked eating disorders with the need to be attractive:

> I know if I was watching television with a bunch of guys and they were saying, like "Hey, wouldn't I like that for my girlfriend" and you have to compare yourself and you feel like a total dog. (C[18])

A woman in her twenties who had overcome teenage anorexic crises, told us:

> I was very confused about what being a woman was; for me, it was *Vogue*. Therapy would have to be about all of that stuff. It's all very well to sit in a little room and say you shouldn't feel this way. But as soon as you walk out, it's all around you again. I don't know how much a therapist can do about that. Intellectually I know it's wrong and all the media barrage is wrong, but I still want to look like that. I think it's really important that therapists address that stuff as well. (C[11])

As I have indicated, feminist therapists do emphasize cultural influences. We interviewed a former client who said this focus was her ticket out of bulimia. She describes her involvement in a group that was feminist in orientation:

> The word "feminist" never came up in the group. But one of the things that this group did, and it is one thing that I found absolutely invaluable—it was my ticket out—was that we started talking about the messages in society. "You have to be thin." All these messages that we were getting from ads on TV, and from radio and movies.
>
> We started talking about that and swapping books, and one of the books we were swapping around was *The Beauty Myth* by Naomi Wolf. So I read it, and I could feel myself getting more and more angry as I went through the book. And that anger was very good because it burned away a lot of the power that these messages have. And burned away a lot of the junk that I was getting. Now I sit down and look at a NutriSystem commercial and all I can think is, "You weasels. You are feeding off our self-esteem. You are deliberately hurting us so that you can sell us band-aid [solutions]." Before that, I would believe [commercials] and feel the anxiety of, "I've got to do what they say." (C[54])

It was not only feminist therapists who took cultural influences seriously. A few others did as well. One of these was a woman psychiatrist who worked primarily with children. Some of her adolescent clients had eating disorders, and for these cases she was inclined to move from her psychoanalytic training to a more culture-centered approach. She was particularly struck by the number of young women who are affected by cultural stereotypes, compared with young men.

There are the psychoanalytic theories and so on—but it's obviously societal pressures, societal expectations of slimness. Those expectations are related to women's changing role in society. There is more pressure to succeed on multiple fronts: With obvious responsibility to childbearing, and I suppose people would say child rearing—that's not necessarily a female responsibility, but it tends to be—and a need to succeed, even in terms of supporting a family. There's a tremendous tumult about all that; there are a lot of pressures. (T[4])

Many therapists, however, ignore these social changes. Some still prescribe love and marriage as a cure for various problems presented by their female clients, including eating disorders. Here is the view an elderly male psychiatrist with a strong psychoanalytic orientation:

In all of the cases I have dealt with in great depth, none of them were fully cured until they were married and had a child; that seems to stabilize everything. Now I must admit that in two cases I'm thinking of, marriage also coincided with graduation from university and some career fulfillment as well, but it seemed to me that falling in love was the best cure or having somebody fall in love with them. I don't quite know which one is more important. Falling in love is a sort of a psychic earthquake. Isn't it a whole turning upside down about one's self-esteem and values? They've opened their eyes to a whole other world. Having a fulfilling relationship with a partner is by far the most curative thing. If we could only arrange that for our anorexics I think they would do an awful lot better.

I've seen one person who had a similar sort of experience. It was a religious conversion when she gave herself to Jesus and the anorexia went away, too. (T[23])

When Causal Conceptions Collide

When underlying factors are discussed but not resolved, it may be difficult (or impossible) for therapist and client to fit their therapy narratives together. A striking example came from interviews with a therapist and one of her former clients.

The therapist was a psychologist with a behavioral orientation. From her experience with clients who suffered from eating disorders, she had come to see family interaction as the central problem. But she had no training in family therapy and preferred not to do it. She would see the client alone but would focus on family dynamics. This suited her belief that eating disorders are an expression of "anger and control." The interviewer asked whether those elements were on the client's side or the parents' side. She answered:

> Both sides. The parents try to control the young people, and young people try to control themselves and their situation by not eating or eating inappropriately. It's a battle of wills between the parents and the kid. (T[6])

How does this approach play out with a client who sees her eating disorder as primarily an attempt to make herself more attractive to men, not a result of family dynamics? The client thought of her problem as a combination of social influence and body image. Although she acknowledged that she had family problems, she did not consider that these problems had much to do with her bulimia. She was upset that the therapist ignored aspects she thought were important:

> She didn't touch on body acceptance with me at all, and that was a big issue with me at the time. She addressed our family life a lot. I think she was saying that the eating disorder was family-stress related. She relied on that a bit too much—the family. She even encouraged me to move out and move in with my boyfriend, much to my mother's dismay. (C[18])

The therapy was a three-session failure, and the client blamed the different conceptions that she and her therapist had concerning the cause of the problem and what could be done to bring about a positive outcome. Two years after her experience with therapy, and without further treatment, the young woman said she simply gave up her bulimia. In her words:

> I think I was just sick and tired of it. I'd had six years of it—six years of dieting and bingeing and purging; and then I said, "Well, frig this. This is boring. I've had enough of it." (C[18])

Some clients we interviewed seemed to have resolved their eating problems. Some had therapy experiences that were effective or simply stopped maladaptive behavior of their own accord. But there were cases in which the clients believed they would never solve the problem.

Sense of a (Bad) Ending

The therapy narrative has a beginning, a middle, and an end—cause, treatment, outcome. This narrative regulates the relationship between therapist and client; therapy cannot happen without it. But that is not to say that therapy always (or even often) has a positive ending. A narrative situation such as the psychotherapy narrative provides a structure within which people can work on problems; it does not ordain actual outcome.

Several clients we interviewed felt that therapy, whatever it did for them, had not cured and would not cure their eating disorders. A university student describes her inpatient experience and her hopelessness about her disorder:

> At the end of two months they said there was really nothing else they could do. I'd gone through the program, but I knew, "I'm not cured." I'd sit there, I wouldn't go to the bathroom and purge, but I was sitting there waiting. If that bathroom door was open, I knew I'd go right away.
>
> So then, when you're getting ready to leave they want to work out some way so you can continue treatment. But I thought "I've had enough of this, this has been two months, just leave it, I don't need anything else." And so I haven't seen a doctor since then. But it's still not over. The way I consider it now, it's just like this is my life. Because I don't think there is any help that anybody can give me now. (C[21])

Even patients who no longer have anorexic episodes or who no longer binge and purge feel they will always be somewhat preoccupied with eating.

> I don't think I'll ever be unneurotic about food. I don't think it goes away at all. I'm still obsessed with weight and dieting. I don't punish myself the way I used to, and I really don't bother dieting, but I always think I should be. (C[11])

Another client, an adult woman, had lost hope of solving her problem with bulimia. She said she had been a fat child who quit school in the ninth grade because she could no longer stand the teasing about her weight. She began to binge and purge, and, despite many treatment attempts, she was still bulimic at the time of the interview.

I know I'll never be better. This is me. That's the way I am. I'll never ever stop, never. Because it's been going on for so long. It's engraved into my life now. It's a part of me. We've tried everything, haven't we? There's not much left to go with, and nothing works. Even if somebody said, "If you're sick one more time you're going to die"—actually they have said that. My esophagus ruptured once—I don't know what they did; they sealed it or something. As soon as they put me on solid foods, I was in the bathroom getting sick again. I just can't help it. It's something I have to do. I was in intensive care. My doctor said, "Why are you doing this?" And I said "Because I don't want to die fat." (C[22])

How do health professionals deal with a case in which the outcome seems to bleak? The client I just quoted talked about the reaction of two physicians in the face of her hopelessness:

He got mad—swore at me—threatened me . . . and that made me really angry and then that's when I took it a step further, I think more for spite. I hated him.

I've got a new doctor now, and in passing he'll say, "So how's the eating disorder going?" I say, "Fine," and he says, "Still doing it?" And I say, "Yup." "When are you going to stop doing this?" "Never." "Okay." (C[22])

Neither of these physicians was a psychotherapist. The client had been in therapy, and she had told therapists that she did not know if she wanted to change.

They forget about it and just go on with something else. I think they just let it go because if something happens that I don't make it, I'm just one person. I'm just a statistic.[laugh]. So I don't think it's really that big of a deal. (C[22])

Not many therapists in our sample share the pessimism of these clients, but some do. A male psychologist was unwilling to talk to clients about his conception of their disorder, because he did not want to share his hopelessness with them.

Hope is a very important component in the relationship; the therapist has to convey hope. I evolve this notion of hope, and we talk about it every session. They want to think they are going to get better and to be told they are going to get better. And I do that. Always. "I think you can do it, you can try." But they don't outgrow it. The manifestation of the eating disorder changes, but intrapsychic dynamics are the same. (T[5])

This therapist has the most chilling of reasons for avoiding full and open discussion with clients: He wants to convey hope that he does not have for them.

Summary

People who suffer from eating disorders are a varied group. Some have one anorexic crisis, become extremely frightened, and do not repeat. Some engage in bulimia as a weight-loss strategy for a period in adolescence and give it up.

But there are others who believe they will never be cured. They expect to turn to their old habits in time of stress, or they think that, even if they give up the clinical symptom, they must resign themselves to a lifelong preoccupation with food and weight. Their pessimism, as we have seen, challenges some therapists' sense of their mission. But even clients who believe they will never be completely "cured" often find benefit and comfort in the therapy relationship. A strong therapeutic alliance helps them come to terms with important features of their lives. And, for some, their preoccupations and symptoms have simply become part of those lives.

When members of this diverse group come into contact with the mental health system, they find many treatment possibilities, many opinions about causal factors, and many negotiating styles. Some therapists ask only for specific consent—"this is what I will do in treatment with you, if you wish." Some talk about alternatives, particularly the options that they themselves feel competent to use with patients. Some envision situations in which they might make a referral to another therapist with different expertise. We found that, whatever their negotiating style, therapists often worry about the downside of presenting a shopping list of alternatives: clients might be overwhelmed by irrelevant information, lose confidence in the therapist, or (when a referral is among the options) feel rejected.

Therapists who deal with this group have another problem: One common belief about the dynamics of eating disorders gives primacy to a battle for control, first between client and family, then between client and therapist or hospital staff. Extensive (or any) negotiation, they think, might feed into what they see as the client's dysfunctional need to control situations. Not all therapists take that view, and few take it with all clients. But even when they do, bypassing the essential elements of in-

formed consent puts them at odds with current legal and ethical requirements.

In chapter 5 we will consider control from a different perspective, looking at the severe lack of control that occurred at the time the client was sexually abused and that continues to be a negative element in the survivor's
life. In these cases, a major treatment task is to build up the client's belief
that she or he has control over life events. This task seems consistent with
full negotiation of therapy options; we will see, however, that with sex
abuse survivors, too, there are many styles of obtaining consent, and many
reasons offered for disclosing or withholding information.

5

■ ■ ■ ■ ■ ■ ■ ■ ■

Survivors of Sexual Abuse

THE HERO of Victor Hugo's *Les Misérables*, Jean Valjean, stole a loaf of break to feed his sister's starving children. This petty crime shaped the hero's whole life. It was an early event that haunted him no matter how he tried to change his circumstances.

There is some parallel with the situation of survivors of sexual abuse. Although what has happened to them is by no means petty or minor, the parallel is the shaping force of a past event whose consequences continue to reappear at various stages of one's life—no matter how much one tries to forget, and no matter how much time passes. Clients who have been sexually abused in childhood often present themselves in therapy with other problems (including substance abuse, relationships problems, and the eating disorders discussed in chapter 4). A therapist may also find that early trauma is still working itself out in current problems. A psychiatrist told us this story about an elderly woman who had suffered for years from periodic depression and lifelong pessimism:

> I've had one patient I've known for twenty-five years now. She was in psychoanalysis with me, and she went through a five-year period during which we uncovered sexual abuse and incest. She then denied it and the denial lasted a year or two, but then she finally admitted it again and then denied

it again. I know her husband, and I know the family, I know the background very well now after all these years. I've kept in touch with her and, yes, I believe it did happen. But even at this late date—she's now in her sixties—she can still hardly bring herself to admit it. (T[23])

As we will see in this chapter, the way in which the consequences of early abuse cycle through later life problems provides some major issues for therapists: How much should they seek out evidence of early trauma when the client has come for a current, different problem in living? And, once the link has been made, which issue should be the focus of treatment, or which should be addressed first?

Before discussing those matters, I will introduce a client whose story has such eerie parallels with Hugo's Jean Valjean that I refer to him as JV. His case differs from the majority of sexual abuse cases in several ways: he is male; abuse occurred throughout early adolescence; the abuser was completely outside the circle of family and family friends; although JV had trouble remembering some aspects of the abuse—the most traumatic memories were the stuff of nightmares—he always knew the broad outlines of what had happened to him. Despite these differences from most cases that therapists see (women clients abused in early childhood by someone in or close to the family, often with repression of the traumatic memories), JV's experience raises many of the fundamental issues that are discussed in this chapter.

JV was a middle-aged man at the time of the interview. When he was eleven years old, his home was destroyed by fire and all the family's possessions were lost, leaving them destitute. They were given temporary lodging in a shelter. One night, while still in the shelter, JV took a walk that led him past a closed store. He was hungry. He broke into the store and stole a loaf of bread, bologna, and mayonnaise. He was caught, held in the local jail, then sent to youth court, where he was sentenced to three years in what was called a "training school."

The abuse started almost immediately. The main offender, a man I will call Karl, was an official with a supervisory position at the training school. In recent years he has been convicted and jailed for abusing many children sentenced to his care. The treatment of youngsters at this institution, and the trials that resulted years later when JV and others finally went to the police, caused a national scandal. The victims were compensated by the government, but, as in JV's case, their lives were scarred beyond any solace that cash compensation could offer.

There are many reasons why children do not report abuse when it is happening. Often the abuser is in the family, and the child needs to reframe the experience to avoid being overwhelmed by the sense of betrayal. Jennifer Freyd (1994, 1996) has outlined a theory of "betrayal trauma" that attempts to explain this cognitive process. Her work on repressed memory is discussed later in this chapter.

Sometimes the abuser is in a position of such power that disclosure by the child is dangerous. This was the case for JV and other victims in the training school. Nevertheless, on one occasion the abuse became so bad that the boys decided to take the risk and report it. But reporting in a closed institution was not easy. JV chose an opportunity when an inspector came to visit. The boys, some of whom had been abused, had to pass by the inspector as they filed into a gymnasium. JV seized his moment:

> Karl was at the head of the line. I had finally gotten up enough nerve. I almost threw my guts up when I ran out of that lineup and ran over to [the inspector] and tried to tell him what happened. I was having trouble getting it all out. He said, "I don't have time to listen to this." And it just seemed like everything fell apart. Like if he didn't want to listen—at that time, for him not to listen to me and to take me to one side and hear what I had to say was devastating. It hurt me a lot because I lost all trust in anyone. So that was the last time I tried to report it until I contacted the police in 1991 [twenty years later]. (C[84])

The failure of inspectors to listen to and follow up on occasional courageous attempts by the boys to report abuse became one of the most notorious features of the later court cases. For JV, the result of trying to report was more abuse, both sexual and physical, which kept him from making any more overt complaints while in the training school. He knew well that he was in a position of complete powerlessness, and he suffered the profound loss of trust in authorities that is common in survivors of childhood sexual abuse.

JV's early admission to the training school had the usual effect of teaching him about crime. After his release, he got into more trouble and spent much of his adolescence in various types of jails. Eventually he tried to put his life in order; he got a job, got married, and had children. When we met him he had had two failed marriages. He believed the problems in his first marriage stemmed from the traumatic abuse, while the failure of his second marriage was a result of disclosure of that abuse and the consequent publicity.

> My [first] ex-wife tried to commit suicide, and she said that I had held a gun to my children's heads and I was gonna blow their brains out. I was arrested and charged with attempted murder—or three attempted murders. They found out a little later on, when my ex-wife came out of a coma [from her suicide attempt], that what she was saying was definitely not the truth, and they dropped the charges.
>
> That's when I started going to see the psychiatrist. Actually, he never really got into the issue of what my ex-wife said or what happened. We never touched on any of those issues, which I thought was really strange because that is why I wanted to see a professional.
>
> I seen him for approximately fifteen years, which did not do a heck of a lot of good. All he ever did was prescribe Valium to calm my nerves down. Then I saw him on a biweekly basis, then it was on a monthly basis, then every six months, and then every year. After that I just stopped seeing him because I wasn't getting anywhere with him. (C[84])

The interviewer asked if the psychiatrist had offered any other treatment alternative besides Valium.

> Yeah, anger management tapes. I still have the one that the psychiatrist gave me many, many years ago. I find it quite useless because there is so much anger inside me and frustration with the system. It's like a cancer inside. (C[84])

This account may be instructive for those who believe that therapists are prone to search for repressed memories of abuse where none exist—an issue I take up later in this chapter. JV was a client with serious current problems that might well have been rooted in the past, especially since he spent his teenage years in institutions. The memories were not entirely repressed. Nevertheless, in a relationship spanning fifteen years, the psychiatrist apparently did little about JV's current problems, nor did he delve into the past. It was JV himself who tried to deal with his own history:

> I started studying psychology and finding out my own answers. That was the only way I could do it; that is when I started really finding out. I would

be down at the library just about every day reading up on different things: sexual abuse, physical, mental, emotional abuse. And law books. (C[84])

His attempts to do therapy on himself included trying to remember all the details of the training school abuse. These came to him while he was sleeping, so he decided to capture his nightmares. He began keeping a tape recorder by his bed, something he still did at the time of our interview.

> I don't have full memory of everything. I can have a nightmare and wake up. I keep a tape recorder right on my nightstand. If I have a nightmare I turn it on and talk.
>
> It is like I am back in the training school in the hole for so long at a time that you don't have any contact with human beings so you start talking to yourself. A lot of these things—they're back in my mind, but they are starting to, gradually and slowly, come out. I can't bring them out in the daytime because I blocked everything off and I shut it out. But at night—the point is, it scares me, the thoughts that I am thinking in my sleep. These are not the thoughts that I would normally think—of hurting anyone. (C[84])

Not all therapy failed for JV. At the time of our interview, he had been working for some time with a psychologist. They were exploring both past and present issues and the possible links between them. JV felt that he had considerable control over where therapy went and that he would have quit if he did not.

> My therapist is a good psychologist, and he gets to the point. But, with me, he has to be very careful what he says because I understand psychology. He knows I studied it while I was in the training school, while I was a kid reading books, and in jail, and in a few other places. And I told [him] this so I could be up front about it. So as not to, for lack of better words, bullshit me. Because I don't like to be bullshitted. So now that he knows this, he is very practical in what he says. He says it straight out. He says, "This is what we have to do. We are either gonna do it or we are not gonna do it. You choose." He puts the cards right on the table and that is what I like about him, because he is doing a good job at it. (C[84])

The interviewer raised the question of whether a male or a female therapist was preferable, since many clients have particular difficulty with therapists of the same sex as the abuser. JV had this difficulty but decided that he needed to overcome it.

I did not feel comfortable with him at first, and I told him that. I wanted to see a female psychologist. He was very positive. He said, "I can understand why you don't want to see a male because you were raped by a male."

I stayed with him because I knew I had to learn somewhere along the line that I had to trust a man. I just did not feel comfortable for the first almost year and a half with my male therapist, and I told him that right up front. I have worked through it, and it was something I never thought I could do. I would never let him sit as close as you [female interviewer] and I are right now. He would sit across a table about four or five feet away from me. I believe I am starting to trust him, and I am trying to let that stone wall come down one piece at a time. (C[84])

Therapy with survivors of sexual abuse is a process of constantly reestablishing a very conditional trust. Despite JV's positive experience with his psychologist, the therapeutic alliance was tenuous and was likely to remain so for a long time.

Sometimes I go into a state like I don't want to see him. Something clicks in my mind and I think, "Why am I even bothering wasting this guy's time and my own time going to see him because this is never going to be resolved inside myself?" It's not his fault. (C[84])

Survivors often face the problem of whether to make a report to police. This may become an issue between therapist and client. In JV's case, however, the need to report came out of his nightmares and his reading. He began to understand the depth of his anger and the need to resolve it. That took him to the police.

The case produced the sort of publicity that seldom accompanies child abuse. Because of what the events said about conditions in facilities for young offenders, there was intense public scrutiny. Television cameras and reporters greeted witnesses each day as they arrived at the courthouse. Testimony was reported in detail. Even though he received monetary compensation and had some sense that an injustice was at last being addressed, JV had decidedly mixed feelings about whether the prosecution was worthwhile.

I divorced my first wife in 1978. I got married again in 1979 and that lasted fifteen years. It all started heading downhill when I came forward with what I had to say. And then my marriage broke down. She couldn't handle the stress of what I was saying out in public. I told her, "What I am gonna be saying—it's not going to be easy on you. But I have got to bring it forward because I know that there is a lot of other guys who have been raped by this guy, and there were other officers in there who were doing some pretty vile things and it has to come out. And if us older guys don't speak up, the younger guys aren't gonna stand a chance."

No, it doesn't always help to file charges. That is the hardest part and that is the most degrading part. It can backfire. It has backfired on myself. Because when I went public with this my ex-wife was so embarrassed—it actually destroyed my marriage. Disclosure is not always the best thing. (C[84])

A common question in any therapy is whether the therapist has an empathic advantage if he or she has suffered or experienced the same problem as the client. Are recovered alcoholics better at working with alcoholics? Does it help a client to know that the therapist has had the same problem? JV believed that a survivor can offer a special understanding. JV was not only a client but a lay therapist. He was coleader of a group I will call Self-Help. Its members were all survivors of sexual and physical abuse in regional institutions like the training school, and many had testified in the trials of former guards. Here is JV, describing the quality of his relationship with these other survivors.

I am able to help people through my own experiences. These people look at me and they trust me because they know I have been through it, being raped and beaten and what have you. And the physical contact—I can actually shake their hand or touch them and they don't back off. Because they can look into my eyes and see what I see in their eyes—the pain and everything that has gone on in their life. (C[84])

His experience as a coleader of a group of male survivors gave us an opportunity to explore another controversial topic with JV: To what extent should group material be kept confidential? For professionals working with survivors, the problem is whether a legal report should be made when an abuser is identified who is still a danger to the public. For those who work with offenders, as we will see in chapter 6, the question is whether offenders themselves should be reported if they disclose abuse they have committed. Although JV's group consisted of survivors, some of them had also become sex offenders. And those offenses were generally not known outside the group. Which takes priority, confidentiality or responsibility to report? For JV, who had suffered so much at the hands of society's control systems, there was no question.

> I don't say anything because I am not in a position to judge anyone. I am not a police officer. These sessions are very private, and we let the person know that we are behind them but what they have done is wrong and, morally you know, it is wrong to do anything like that. But we let them judge themselves. It does come up. Quite often. But like we tell them, "We are not the judge and jury here. We cannot judge you. So if you, in the future, want to bring it out or someone has you charged, you will go through it. But that will come with time." (C[84])

This ethical stance is very different from that prescribed for professionals in the human services. The interviewer asked JV whether his feeling would change if he knew that the group member was describing current and ongoing sexual offenses against children.

> It does change. I mean, if it happened in the past and they are getting help for it, that is fine. But if it is still on a continuing basis, I take them aside or [the coleader] will take them aside and just say, "Listen, you know you have to do something about this now before it goes any further and if it is still going on, you have got to stop." We can't go to the police because of the confidentiality, but we advise them to seek more psychological help, let their psychologist know, and go see the police and report it themselves. That is a very difficult thing to do because they know what might happen. They may end up in prison. (C[84])

Despite his uneasiness about what he hears from group members, JV maintains confidence. The mistrust of the system is so great that survivors like JV believe they must use their own resources—books, self-help groups—and maintain what trust they can among themselves.

JV's story highlights a number of themes about treatment of survivors of child sexual abuse that recur in this chapter. The extreme lack of control that the abuse victim suffers and the need to reestablish that control in the therapeutic context encourage negotiation. Lack of control is related to lack of trust, making the establishment and maintenance of the therapeutic alliance of primary importance.

Similarities between therapist and client are often an issue in therapy. In all three problem areas discussed in this book, there is some argument to be made (and some clients make it) that a therapist who has not had the problem cannot fully understand clients who do have it. Another similarity issue in treating survivors is the question of the sex of therapist. Some therapists argue that the survivor must learn to deal with people of the same sex as the abuser, and they suggest that the best place to do that may be in the (relative) safety of psychotherapy. Other therapists agree with clients who are adamant about having a therapist who does not remind them of the abuser.

Then there is the question of whether therapy should focus on past abuse or current problems. JV had a fifteen-year therapy experience in which he felt he made no progress. He believed that only when he began to deal with past trauma on his own, through his reading, did he begin to understand where his current problems came from. This question of past versus present is one that divides therapists. The therapist's willingness to search for past material that the client does not spontaneously report (or, in some cases, even seem to remember) leads us to the controversy over repressed memories versus false memory syndrome.

To disclose in therapy and to disclose to the police are different matters. This survivor believed that his life was made worse by legal disclosure. He had no interest in breaking confidentiality in his self-help group. The question of making a legal report becomes, we will see, another issue for negotiation.

Negotiating Consent

This book is a survey of the terrain covered by therapists and clients as they negotiate informed consent. Although it is not primarily an evaluation of therapist's procedures, I noted at the outset that I would identify some descriptions of negotiation that seem exemplary.

The next two therapists described the sort of thoughtful, control-sharing negotiation that fits the conception of therapy advanced in this book. Both are women psychologists. One identifies herself as a feminist therapist; the other is a cognitive constructivist. One is a university professor with a private practice; the other is a clinician in a large teaching hospital. Both deal with a variety of problems but have a substantial number of clients who are survivors of sexual abuse.

The first therapist is one of two book authors among the therapists we interviewed. She is the coauthor of a book on feminist therapy. Some years

ago she began a private practice, in addition to her faculty position, because she thought there was a demand for therapists with her conceptual
position. Here is how she describes her approach to the negotiating
process:

> I let them tell their story in their own words and in their own time. I have a
> variety of techniques that may be helpful, but I'm always handing power
> over to the client. The client makes a decision as to what it is she wants to
> work on and how she'd like to work on it, the pace at which she wants to
> work, and so on. I'm constantly learning from my clients.
>
> I encourage my clients to be conscientious consumers of the service and
> so I invite them to ask questions—about me, about my practice, about any-
> thing that I do. I want that to be ongoing because I don't see *me* as the ex-
> pert on *their* experience. I see me as a person who has particular skills that I
> can bring to them. But they have the expertise on themselves.
>
> They have to feel safe enough to do this kind of work, so we'd always start
> from the place of safety. I will say, "What would you like to work on today?"
> If they can identify the issue, then we go to their safe place and I ask them
> again. Because sometimes, when you've relaxed, it could have turned out to
> be something else, so I always ask again before we get started, "Now is this
> the issue that you want to deal with, and are you ready?"
>
> I don't set the agenda; they do. I've had people who have chosen not to
> go through therapy because they find it too scary or they don't think they're
> ready, and I respect that. [They may say] "No, look, I really don't want to
> do this," and then they don't come to therapy any more. They'll withdraw.
> (T²⁷)

The second therapist whose negotiation has exemplary qualities has a hospital-based practice. Her clients are often suffering from some adult problems associated with trauma, often the trauma of childhood sexual abuse.
She considers herself a constructivist. This school of therapy believes that
people impose cognitive classifications on events in order to understand
their world and that such classifications affect what events they recall and
the way they recall them. She leavens her constructionism with Beck's
(1991) cognitive approach—helping clients recognize the way irrational
thinking defeats their purposes. Here she describes negotiating with
clients:

> I am very clear with patients when they are referred that I am going to see
> them for a few sessions to do an assessment for therapy. They know that I am

going to be asking them a lot of questions about what the issues are and what difficulties they are dealing with. I find out whether they have had past therapy, what their response was to past therapy, what things have helped, what things haven't helped, and generally what their coping strategies are. We look at what they want to deal with and what they might gain from therapy at this point in their life.

I will also be very clear about my rationale with respect to therapy. What I am really doing is looking at the client and assessing what their difficulties are, looking at their suitability for therapy, whether there is anything that I feel as a therapist I can offer them, and then, in terms of my approach, is this a match or not?

At the end of that assessment, which may be three to five sessions, the patient and I will sit down and talk about my perceptions and what I think they are looking at in terms of therapy. They will also provide me information. And I'll basically say, "Well, this is what I could offer you. I would be willing to see you over x number of sessions focusing on these issues, and this is generally the approach that we'll be taking."

I would let them know that at the end of that number of sessions we will review where we are. I will have my own perceptions at that point, too—but just opening up the dialogue, a therapy review in terms of where we are; how the person has been making out; what things have been helpful; what are some of the other issues if any that he or she would like to deal with; or where we are with the issues that we started to deal with; whether it makes sense to go on for further sessions at that point or to take a break, or to consider referral to a different therapist with a different approach or orientation.

But the alliance is essential, and the match is very important. If you are trying to do cognitive therapy approach with an individual who says, "Well, I never had a conscious thought before the age of thirty," chances are they are not going to be very amenable to cognitive therapy if they can't access any thoughts. (T[60])

Neither of these two therapists feels she can help all clients. Both know their own orientations and explain them to clients, but they know that they are not for everyone. They engage in mutual assessment that involves therapist and client.

One problem that faces therapists as they try to negotiate is how to deal with clients who have very different backgrounds from those of the therapists. Negotiation ultimately requires that therapist and client use the same terms to mean the same things; if the client learns those terms from the therapist, there remains a doubt about whether agreements are the result of true negotiation or of clients learning to talk with a therapy voice.

One therapist discussed the problem posed by differences in educational level and the possibility that clients may misunderstand therapy. This was a female psychologist who spent an internship working with students at a university counseling center. She then went to work for a regional health service in a rural area, where she found a very different client population. She talked about the difficulty of bridging the education gap, and in particular about addressing her rural clients' unrealistic expectations of psychotherapy.

> Those I work with, they are really disenfranchised. Poor, poor folks who don't probably have access to magazines. A couple of times people have come in saying, "I think this might have happened to me before the age of one year. I want to find out if it did in therapy." And essentially impossible tasks like that. If they could get the memory, life would be okay.
>
> If your life is a mess, retrieving your memory won't necessarily make it okay. And you still have to deal with some scars that abuse has left in your life. Healing the scars goes beyond remembering whether it happened or not. Sometimes these are people who are saying, "I want to remember this one abuse incident." But they have got a hundred thousand abuse incidents that they *do* remember—molestation when they were teenagers and so on— and they don't want to work on those. They want to find this one that happened before they were the age of one. And so sometimes there is a naive notion about what therapy for sexual abuse will involve. (T[80])

It was common for therapists we interviewed to have different slants on negotiations in therapy depending on the perceived ability of their clients to understand what therapy can and cannot do. We asked another therapist with a rural practice who described herself as a feminist therapist how she addresses the question of choices with clients who have little understanding of therapy.

> I don't know if I address it. Because, when I get to know the person, I guess I have sort of an intuition as to whether they're a more cognitive person, a more feeling type of person, what their imagination is like.
>
> I remember reading that doing therapy was like having a ring of keys, and the therapist's job is to pick up each key and very gently try it in the lock and see if this one works and, if not, put it back and take up the next one. That's

what I'm doing with the person, based on my sense of what type of person they are, what their makeup is, what their strengths are, how healthy they are.

So it's not a matter of there being different techniques or approaches or philosophical stances as much as it is my sense or my courage or my willingness or my daring or whatever it is to be creative and to try a lot of different things with this person to see what's helpful. (T[14])

There is little negotiation in this therapist's approach. It is the therapist's intuition, the therapist's creativity, the therapist's courage that are relied upon. You may be surprised that this therapist calls what she does feminist therapy, since it seems at odds with some other versions presented here of what is also called feminist therapy. Our interviews with therapists showed that their techniques differed considerably even though they used the same formal labels for their work. Marecek and Kravetz (1998) found these same discontinuities in their interview research with one hundred self-identified feminist therapists.

For a different feminist perspective, I return to the book author I quoted earlier. She told us there are philosophical reasons for encouraging clients, especially women clients, to take an active part in negotiation throughout treatment.

Women have been socialized to defer to authority, to not challenge authority. They come in and they see this man [who says], "Okay, we'll give you a battery of tests. Right, you come out on this scale. Here's what's wrong. This is what you need. This is what's wrong with you. I am going to fix you up."

We've been socialized as females to defer anyway, [to think] that our opinions are less valuable, that we don't really know best, that experts know best, and so forth. Women are much less likely to challenge that point of view even if they think, "But that doesn't feel right for me, or this isn't feeling good for me, or I'm not feeling better about this." They still think, "Well, yeah, but he's the expert, he must know what he's doing." (T[27])

Trust and Control

Sexual abuse survivors were often abused by the very adults whom they trusted to protect them. As a result, they suffered a sense of betrayal and a traumatic loss of control. A significant component of therapy is reestablishing a trusting relationship with an authority figure. Encouraging the client to take as much control as possible in therapy seems to be one of the keys to the healing process. We interviewed a feminist therapist who made a blunt comparison between loss of control during abuse and that during therapy.

> Choice is the thing that is taken away. When someone is abused they don't have a choice, especially when they are a child. Being forced to touch your uncle's penis or being forced to tell a therapist about doing it—in both cases, you are being forced. You are doing something against your will. What is critical is that your choice is taken away from you. (T[63])

For a client's view of the importance of having choices, I introduce a woman who had been sexually abused at the age of twelve by someone outside the family. She saw a psychologist at a trauma center and, later, a holistic therapist, and she reflected on the two experiences:

> The therapist at the sexual assault center—I was just in knots before I went to see her. It was very much like, "Okay, sit down and now, whether you feel like it or not, you have to talk about this. And you're only allowed to talk about this, and you're not allowed to talk about anything else." I thought that there were some other issues that I needed to talk about that were sort of related. She said, "I'm sorry, unless you want to talk specifically about the sexual abuse, I'm not going to talk to you." I don't see how therapy can be in isolation. You can't take one event out of somebody's life and just say, we can't look at anything else.
>
> That was just really uncomfortable, unhelpful. I really have questions about her competence. She made suggestions, and she told me what to do instead of letting me figure it out, or letting me ask questions. (C[11])

She stopped seeing that therapist, but since she still felt she needed help she started again with someone who called herself a holistic therapist. Although she found the therapist a bit strange, the client said there was much more give-and-take in this relationship.

> The holistic therapist, I thought some of the stuff she did was flaky. She didn't do it with me, because I sort of said, "That's flaky!" But I felt incredibly comfortable with her. I just felt like it was a safe place where I could say any-

thing. I could say whatever I felt, and she might say, "Well, does that really make sense?" or whatever. I could say it, because I really trusted her. (C^{11})

One issue that may be related to building trust is the sex of therapist. JV, who was abused by males, found it hard to trust a male authority figure. Male therapists may also be distrusted by women whose abusers were men. Here is a comment from a forty-year-old woman whose father abused her:

> The hardest thing for me to do is to trust somebody. I don't have a lot of friends, because it's just really hard for me to trust. I never trusted a man until I met my boyfriend. And we were friends before anything else—I think that's what made the difference. (C^{41})

The importance of this issue is illustrated by an interview with a client who had been sexually tormented by her father. Later, she developed an eating disorder, which tended to be the sole focus of therapy. But, at the same time, problems with her father were continuing. His behavior when she was a young adult finally drove her to a psychiatric ward.

> It was a lot of innuendo stuff and exhibitionism and some fondling when he was drunk. Things like, you know, "Gee, you're really blossoming and it really is too bad you're my daughter." And of course implicit in that was, "If you weren't my daughter, then I could fuck you."
>
> When he left my mother, he married a woman the same age as me. My partner and I went to visit, and my father was still continuing his really crazy sexual kinds of things, and he proposed that we swap, you know, he with me and my partner with his wife.
>
> And then that Christmas he came to visit, and there was an incident where we were dancing and he did this whole thing again of, "Gee, you know, you're really beautiful, and it really is too bad you're my daughter." And he had a hard-on and was rubbing it up against me. It was just before I went into the hospital—I really sort of fell apart after that and ended up in the psych ward.
>
> It did absolutely nothing for my problems. Didn't address them. But I really liked being there—I was having great success with losing weight, and I got lots of attention. Throughout my life I learned or I believed that when I was sick people cared about me, and when I wasn't, people didn't. (C^{33})

Her story points to an iatrogenic side of health care. People who feel that no one cares for them may find that they are of interest only when they are displaying symptoms. The importance of the sex of therapist and of group members, and the insensitivity with which the issue may be handled in the health system, are also features of this case.

> When I was discharged from the hospital, I had to participate in this post-discharge group. This is after finally saying that "I think there was probably some sexual abuse that I needed to deal with and blah blah blah." They put me in a discharge group with nine men and two male facilitators and I was the only female. It was a disaster. It was a totally ridiculous, useless experience, but it was one of the conditions of my discharge. (C[33])

In therapy generally, there has been some study of sex match between client and therapist (see Tanney and Birk, 1976). But the issue of matching sex is of particular concern when the problem is childhood sexual abuse. Here, the question becomes the sex of therapist and of abuser. We asked about the importance of sex of therapist when we interviewed a client who had a history of abuse by multiple offenders in her family.

> It depends on who the abuser was, I think. Almost all the women I know would never talk with a man. I have a handful of friends that are male survivors, and they'd rather wait for two years on a waiting list than they would go see an available male. (C[47])

A woman psychologist agreed that people abused by a male have difficulty working with a male therapist, even though some therapists manage to deal successfully with the issue.

> There are male therapists who are so talented and gifted that quickly the issue resolves itself. The good therapists address it right off. "I am a male. How does that make you feel? What are your worries? Are there any concerns about that?" We talk about people needing to feel safe enough to explore things. But if they just can't do it with a male, one should honor the request for a female, because it is really important that they feel safe. (T[80])

On the other hand, some therapists believe an abuse victim can benefit from having a therapist who is the same sex as the abuser. They believe the client needs to learn that relationships with such a person can be positive.

That was JV's opinion when he decided to stick with a male therapist. We heard the same view offered by a female psychologist who used learning theory. In her view, exposure deconditions clients to their fears. Having a therapist of the same sex as the abuser permits the client to rebuild a trusting relationship that has been lost.

A young male psychiatrist working in public mental health agreed that clients may be helped by a therapist of the same sex as the abuser. But he was wary of the ethical and legal complications that might result from such an interaction.

> A male therapist can be quite beneficial to a female sex abuse survivor; therapy properly handled by a male therapist can present a model to a woman that perhaps she has never had before—a model of somebody who is interested and caring and can act in a nonexploitative way—without expecting something in return.
>
> On the flip side, I have had some problems with transference issues with female survivors. I think they need to test to see whether at some point I will behave as their abusers have in the past.
>
> It could potentially be dangerous. Transference issues are very strong, and at times not all that subtle. A person could, out of anger, lay a complaint. Therapy is such a secluded thing. You do it in an office with just the two of you. I am as unprotected as the client. If there was an accusation, I have no way to prove that I did or didn't do a particular thing. (T[59])

Not all survivors are female, of course, and not all offenders are male. With regard to female offenders: As we might expect, survivors who have been abused by a woman have trouble trusting a female therapist. This point was made by a female social worker who specialized in treating adolescents who are offenders but who have also been victims of abuse.

> Many of the boys have been abused by a female, or they have a history of sort of an emotional incestuous relationship with a female caregiver. Either way, their experience of females has not been good. (T[79])

We found some clients who thought that it helped the therapy process if the therapist was also a survivor of abuse, although clients realized it would be unrealistic to expect that background in a therapist. One appeal of groups like JV's Self-Help is that leaders have experienced abuse. They have, in JV's view, an empathy impossible in one who has not been through the experience. A similar sentiment about therapist empathy was expressed by a female client:

> That's one of the biggest problems [my therapist] and I had. She's not a survivor, and I had a real problem with that. She kept saying, "Oh, I understand, I understand"—you bloody well don't understand. No, you don't. Unless you've been there, you do not understand. You can empathize, you can sympathize, you can imagine, but you can't *know*. (C[47])

So far I have discussed trust as an issue between a client and a therapist. But trust can also involve the whole mental health system. We interviewed a woman who was in charge of the psychology program in a health delivery service. She talked about how the system itself can undermine client confidence.

> The more a person has been burned by a system, the harder it is for them to develop a relationship. If people have had early diagnoses—and some have had diagnoses since adolescence and have been on inpatient units—the longer that they have suffered, the longer it takes to develop rapport. The earlier the person was misdiagnosed, the more difficult it is for them to be functional and to benefit from treatment. If they came to anybody's attention twenty-five years ago, they would have been misdiagnosed because nobody was trained to even see these problems. (T[68])

Next I take up an issue that is often a source of friction between therapists and survivors of sexual abuse: whether survivors should press charges against their abusers.

Pressing Charges

The question of whether to encourage clients to approach legal authorities is a nettlesome one. The abuser may still pose a threat, if not to the client, then to others. The therapist may feel pressure to do something about that threat. When the client does not agree, it again brings up the issue of who controls what is happening in the therapy relationship.

Life is not easy for clients who become entangled with the legal system. JV, you will recall, felt his life was ruined by reporting the training school abuse. A feminist therapist said that those difficulties are the reason she was not interested in working in what the police and prosecutors define as the public interest. She puts her relationship with the client first

> The police will sometimes refer someone to me. The client will have made an informal complaint to the police but not a formal one. The police would somehow think that my job was to work for them to get the person ready to make the formal complaint. And I would say: "No, my job is to work with the person and help them make a decision about how they want to deal with it." It is fine with me if they decide to go forward; it is fine with me if they decide not to go forward. I am not working for the police. (T[63])

When the therapist feels an ethical obligation to see that authorities are notified but the client does not want to report, the result can be a tug of war that undercuts the therapeutic alliance. Here again is the twenty-year-old who suffered multiple sexual abuse in her family and even had a child by her father. She told us she had never made a legal report.

> My therapist and I discussed it because she's sort of pro charges, but at this point in my life it wouldn't benefit me at all. It would hurt a lot of people. And, besides, whenever anyone presses charges, it's always the victim who's on trial, and I don't want to go through that.
>
> My therapist respects my opinion. She may not agree with it. She's never been one to pressure me into doing anything. Well, she has tried a couple of times and then she hasn't seen me for months on end, so she knows what it does. Ultimately, I'm the only one that really knows what's best for me. (C[47])

The more therapists know about the legal system, the less likely they seem to be to encourage reporting. The supervisor of a psychological service told us she was pessimistic about what survivors undergo when they lay charges.

> There is always a feeling that on the witness stand that they will be seen as the person to blame. And they can't handle that real deep belief that they were bad somehow. Public notoriety, too. Having to go to court is a matter of public record. Also a belief that family members will turn against them as they were perceived to have done when they were children. There are some people who really aren't well enough or strong enough to be able to go through all those things. I used to see children, and I had a duty to report.

I can't tell you the number of children who told me later that they wished I'd never reported because their life had been hell since. And they saw the whole thing as a horrible adversarial attack against them. You tell them, "You have disclosed this to me. I have to report it now. And here is what's going to happen." And what is going to happen to them is quite terrible; you can't begin to prepare them for it. (T[68])

There are other cases in which survivors want to report because they expect more than the legal system will give, or they expect more catharsis than is realistic. A female social worker who knew the legal system well—she had worked in the probation service and in prisons—felt she had an obligation to tone down the expectations of survivors who were enthusiastic about reporting.

When someone is first remembering that they were sexually abused there is a lot of rage, there is hurt, there is confusion. I think it is important to work through that or work with that for a period of time and allow the person to decide for him or herself, "What do you want to do with this? If you were to charge so-and-so for something that happened to you fifteen years ago, these are the possibilities: Nothing, he may get nothing. It may be dismissed. He may be found guilty and get a suspended sentence. Or he may go to the penitentiary." You have to prepare the person for the outcome and let them know it is never going to be enough, whatever the sentence is.

I prefer to allow the person to make up their own mind. I have been working with some women for about a year now, and they are still undecided. They are still very angry, but they have given up any idea that this person is going to the penitentiary, or be castrated, or any of those things. They are saying, "I just want to have my day in court. I just want to face my abuser and tell him what he did to me, and how it hurt, and that I didn't deserve it. And to have the court find him guilty even if he never goes to jail." And I see that as being more real than someone who says, "I want this person to rot in jail for the next twenty years." I know that that isn't going to happen. (T[85])

Beyond therapeutic value for the client, the therapist may feel an ethical responsibility to get the matter into the legal system. The same social worker talked about the ethics of the matter:

The other issue has to do with if the offender is still in a position where he has to access to other children. I am concerned about that, and I will express that to the victim. I will say, you know, "I am concerned that this person still works driving a school bus or works at Boy Scouts, or whatever." That is a real issue for me. But I have to think, what is it that I am to do here without destroying the confidentiality of my client? (T^{85})

Although professionals face this dilemma, as we saw earlier, it is not so acute for abuse victims who have become lay therapists, like JV. He knew the legal system very well; it provided the setting for his abuse and later for the public trials that, in the end, he saw as harmful. With that background, he was not interested in choosing the legal system over trying to help survivors.

Presenting Alternatives

In chapter 4 we saw that there are a variety of approaches advocated for treating eating disorders, depending in part on the therapist's view of the underlying problem. There is no such arsenal of specific treatments in the case of survivors of childhood sexual abuse. The one treatment that has traditionally been associated with recovery of repressed memories is hypnosis.

As classically practiced, hypnosis poses problems for consent in psychotherapy. Cheryl Malmo (1990) has talked about the authoritarian overtones of classical hypnosis. We found various opinions about the risks and benefits of hypnosis for sexual abuse survivors. There are those who believe that it is the most likely treatment to cause false memories, an issue I take up later in this chapter. Whether or not that is true, feminist therapists such as Malmo, who are very concerned about giving control to the client, note that free and informed consent is hard to imagine in a situation where the client is in the suggestible state associated with hypnosis. When we interviewed those who practice traditional hypnosis, they usually argued that they gained consent before using hypnosis. That, however, precludes the sort of ongoing consent that is being urged on health professionals by legal experts (e.g., Rozovsky and Rozovsky, 1990).

One of the problems therapists face is the influence of popular culture. Some people see talk shows that deal with repressed memories and come to therapy convinced that they have had similar experiences and should be hypnotized to search for similar memories. The psychological services supervisor told us about the influence of talk shows.

> I have had several people come and want to be hypnotized. I don't do that. It is not my training. There are people in the mental health system who have a great deal of training in hypnotherapy, but even they are reticent to use that modality because of all of the issues surrounding it right now. There are people who come with a specific "Yes I want to be hypnotized, and I want to find my repressed memories." I try to refer them to someone who can do that for them. Right away. There is no need to hang on to someone who wants a different type of treatment. (T[68])

There are other forms of hypnosis that are less authoritarian than the classical approach. One version is combined with feminist therapy. In this approach, as Malmo describes it, hypnosis is seen as "a natural state of consciousness, a state of deep relaxation combined with heightened concentration and awareness" (1990, p. 196). Control of the trance state is assumed to remain with the client, and the therapist is simply a facilitator. In this use of hypnotic techniques, feminists believe that there is no violation of the need for clients to experience their own power.

A feminist therapist talked about the way she tries to maintain client control of therapy—including hypnosis.

> They may say, "I don't feel comfortable with this." I've had people who are not comfortable doing ego-state work or who don't like the idea of hypnosis. Fine, so we do something else. There are so many different ways to get at it; it doesn't have to be a "technique." Although I must admit that hypnosis is an effective one if people are willing to do it. But some people just don't feel good with that, so that's fine. (T[27])

Although there is not a wide array of techniques that target the effects of sexual abuse, there are some choices available. I have already presented some of them: whether to avoid a match between sex of therapist and abuser and whether to press charges. Another issue that may be the subject of negotiation about how therapy will proceed is the question of how to treat a person who comes to therapy with a current problem and a (possible) history of childhood abuse: Which should the therapist deal with?

The situation in which an abuse survivor comes for help with some other problem is reasonably common. These other problems can include substance abuse, an eating disorder, or difficulty sustaining relationships. The questions that arise are: Which problems should be treated first? Which should be the focus of treatment? Should the therapist insist on dealing with a problem that the client is avoiding? This is, at least in theory, fertile ground for negotiation.

A feminist therapist had many patients who had eating disorders but who had also experienced childhood sexual abuse. She advocated working on the underlying issue, past trauma, rather than on the eating disorder itself. In her opinion, an eating disorder or some other complex of symptoms may be a necessary coping mechanism for the client. It cannot be resolved while it is still serving some function.

> Some would come with an eating disorder and not recognize or even be aware of the fact that there had been abuse in their childhood. The way I look at the issue is not as an eating disorder problem but as a strategy that's been used to somehow compensate for whatever has been going on within the context of the abuse. If the eating disorder is not life-threatening, it doesn't become my major focus.
>
> One of the ways I think about it that if someone's had an accident and their foot is damaged, you don't ask them to throw away the crutch until the leg is healed. As we work through to the [abuse], the other stuff starts taking care of itself. We may talk about [the eating disorder] often because it's an issue, or we may look at it because that's what the client wants to do. But my own view is it's not really going to work itself through until we get to the basis of the abuse and do that. (T[27])

She noted that not all feminist therapists would agree with her. Some prefer to work in the here-and-now, rather than explore the past. But she maintained that nothing important will happen in therapy until the abuse is dealt with. Even so, she said she leaves the matter up to the client. She gives her point of view, indicates that not everyone shares it, and she and the client then work on whichever problem the client chooses.

One therapist who prefers to work with the client's current problem was a male psychologist in a university counseling center. He said that treatment goals need to be more precise than just coming to terms with some past event.

> I often think we need to have more specific treatment goals than just getting over sexual abuse. I mean, what does that mean in concrete terms? That boils down to some exploration of how it affects them, and, therefore, what specific changes they want to make. What does it mean to get over sexual abuse—does it mean not thinking about it any more? Maybe not that. Does

it mean never feeling angry about it? It may not mean that either. Or does it mean being able to have a normal sexual life? Maybe it's that. Maybe it means being able to not feel so interpersonally anxious. Maybe it means being able to see oneself as normal with other people—acceptable, likable, that sort of thing. (T[9])

A woman psychologist who saw many substance abusers who were also survivors of abuse argued that therapists should focus on the problem presented by their clients.

> I think you have to pay a lot of attention to what the person's initial complaint is. You have to validate that. It is also important that you keep your eyes open for [other issues]. But that has to be balanced with not wanting to fit your model onto a particular client that you are seeing. (T[69])

There is some concern that therapists may get involved in an abuse history before the client is ready. A female psychologist worked with troubled adolescents—often street kids. She told us that it is important to deal with current issues and to establish a good relationship before delving into a history of sexual abuse.

> Regardless of whether they are a survivor or not, safety and stabilization is the first phase of any therapy. If someone is in crisis, if someone is slashing themselves, if someone is eating disordered to the point where they are really endangering their health, if they're on the run, if they are in an abusive relationship with a man, there is the risk of destabilizing someone even more if you focus on really intense issues too soon. I target things that are destroying their coping at that moment and leave the survivor issues until the person can really do them.
>
> The danger is that you would stir something up while they are in a life of chaos. They are hurting themselves, being promiscuous, driving their cars recklessly, drinking a lot—because they can't tolerate the emotion that they experience. They need to learn, in therapy, how to tolerate strong emotion in a more adaptive way before they can go on to handle the strong emotions they will feel when you pursue the sexual abuse issues. (T[80])

Even when the client is ready, not all therapists are willing to probe the past for sexual abuse. An elderly psychiatrist thought that people often invent histories of abuse and that, even if the histories are true, people make too much of them. He said this was just a way for clients to avoid taking responsibility for their lives.

> There are people who, because they have been or claim to have been sexually abused, think that that excuses everything and the world owes them a living ever afterwards. Everything in the world would be beautiful if this hadn't happened to them—this should be cured for them. We often have to say to somebody, "Look, the fact that you were sexually abused is not in itself an illness. It's your way of dealing with it that constitutes an illness."
>
> It's the same way as saying, "Look, maybe you had a car accident as a child, and maybe a your mother dropped you on your head, or maybe you were abandoned for a day or two, or maybe you had to go into an orphanage. These are not illnesses. These are incidents in your life that you have to deal with."
>
> People come and say, "I was sexually abused as a child. What are you going to do about it?" We say, "Okay, so these things happened to you. How are you going to deal with it, and what do you intend to make of your life?" Some people want to make themselves into perpetual injuries. (T[23])

Clients who feel a need to work through past abuse might find negotiation with this therapist rather difficult.

So far, I have quoted therapists who talked about the focus of therapy largely as a pragmatic issue. But it can also be seen more broadly as an ethical problem. This was recognized by a female psychologist who had published research on the ethical issues that psychologists face in their practices. She had considerable experience with survivors of sexual abuse, especially teenaged girls, and she had worked with many problem families. She worried about whether the therapist has any right to try to fix problems the client did not bring for help. Is it legitimate for a therapist to try to change the client's values to more closely match those of the therapist?

> Let's say you espouse feminist ideals, but you're working with a family who wants to maintain a traditional lifestyle. If you are fine with that, and you can treat them as that, then I don't think that is a problem—that the politics and values are not the same. I do hold feminist values, but I don't want to stick that on my clients. If a family is happy with the way things are, who am I to come in and muck it up?

> Just because they come to see me, does that mean that they are giving consent for me to fix whatever I think is wrong? I don't think so. If they're saying this isn't a problem, it's none of my business to go in there and say "yes, it is."
>
> I do try to talk to [clients] on where I'm coming from in therapy, what my perspective is, and what I think their role will be and what my role as a therapist would be. I suppose in that way I'm giving some indication of what my politics or my values are. But I think I'm somebody who isn't going to try to fix problems that aren't any of my business to fix. I'm not going to be using my values as a yardstick, saying, "This is a right way to be, and if you're not that way, then there is a problem." (T[17])

Finally, on the question of alternatives, I want to raise the touchy issue of referral. Most therapists we interviewed talked about options in terms of what they could do for a patient. But what happens when the client seems to need something beyond the therapist's own scope?

Referral and Rejection

Some treatment options require a therapist to suggest that a client be seen by someone else. A common theme among therapists was their fear that the client might feel rejected when referral was suggested. We had a chance to explore this situation in a trio of interviews: with a client, with the therapist who referred her, and with the therapist to whom she was referred.

The client was a woman in her thirties who, at the time of her interview, was a year away from being ordained. As a minister, she intended to work on social justice and advocacy issues. While she was in therapy with a male psychologist for other problems, she remembered abuse she had suffered as a child.

> My first memories were memories of terror living in this neighborhood. The sexual abuse probably began at about age three and went on to about age five. It stopped when my family moved away. It was abuse from outside of the family.
>
> The last incident I recall was a neighbor. He was in the navy. I didn't know him well; his wife had agreed to take me out on Halloween one evening. When she picked me up, she had been drinking. She ended up taking me to a store and buying me treats and then back to their house where

they continued to drink and he—I think his was probably the worst—I think that was the only incident that there was vaginal penetration. (C[65])

The client was seen occasionally for chronic, low-level depression. In these contacts with health professionals, there was no attempt to probe her past for possible causes. She described her interaction with two psychiatrists and her family doctor.

> The first psychiatrist gave me a one-hour grilling. He had four pages of notes typed up, and he mailed them off to my family physician after the first session without my consent. My family doctor said, "I have this report." He said, "I haven't even read it all because I don't need to know all of this." I saw the psychiatrist again one month later and it was an eleven-minute session. He had asked me to read, David Burn's book *Feeling Good*.
>
> I went to another psychiatrist and had about three or four sessions with him. He said, "I don't think that you are dealing with anything that you need me for. I'll write and tell your doctor that." And that's the way it went. (C[65])

The client began seeing the male psychologist, someone she had known socially for some time. He was interested in the fact that she had no current romantic interest.

> For two or three years he focused on how to get me involved with a man—suggesting personal ads, "you could hire a match maker . . . we've got to get you a man." He didn't totally miss the abuse, but it seemed to take an awful long time for those issues to come up. (C[65])

When the abuse did become the focus of therapy, the male psychologist suggested she see a woman. Here is the client's perspective on the referral:

> It was obvious that there was more work to be done. Anger was something that I totally suppressed. I could talk very calmly [about the abuse]. I could feel the pain, and the tears would come, and the sadness and the hurt and the grief of it all, but I hadn't felt the anger. He said, "I think you need to work with a woman." I hadn't been overwhelmingly looking for a change. He suggested that I needed a woman's perspective. He said, "You need to be empowered by another woman to get through this."
>
> He realized that there were some things, as a man, that he just couldn't do for female clients. He said, "Give it a try. If it doesn't work, I'm here. See

how it goes." I came in the next week and met with her. It clicked immediately for me. (C^{65})

Although this sounds like a smooth transition, the client told us that she did feel the rejection that many therapists worry about when they consider making a referral.

> When he suggested that I see her and when he [earlier] suggested I see a psychiatrist, there was really a sense of rejection. Both of them happened at major times when I was ready to go forward. And by suggesting "somebody else needs to deal with it," I just felt it was total rejection. I was ready to do the work, and he cut me off at the knees. (C^{65})

In our interviews with the two therapists, we found they used two very different styles of therapy.

The female psychologist, who was still the client's therapist at the time of the interview, was a feminist therapist who specialized in clients who had suffered abuse, either in the past or in current relationships. Early in therapy she labeled abusive experiences and told clients about her feminist orientation.

> Before someone can change their behavior, they have to understand it. Some people get upset and leave therapy as soon as I call it [the behavior] abusive. One of the first jobs of a feminist therapist is to name abuse when she sees it. I am up front about my perspective and how I see things.
>
> I describe myself as a feminist quite early on. Some people are surprised, and they say, "Are you one of those feminists?" [laugh] And I would say, "Yes, and I will tell you what that means to me, and if you don't want to find out any more about that, perhaps you should go somewhere else." (T^{63})

When this therapist describes the main focus of her therapy as "abusive relationships," she defines abuse broadly, as power imbalance in a patriarchal society. She believes that men are victims of that society as much as women and that men can be abused as well as abusers.

> My view of the world is that no matter how a person is being abused, whether it is sexually abused, physically abused, financially abused—the most potent part of the abuse is the psychological. That is the common thread of all the abuses. Broken bones heal, but the damage to self is more lasting. (T^{63})

Despite her initial feelings of rejection, the client seemed happy with her referral to this therapist at the time we interviewed her. The male psychologist, to our surprise, was now thoroughly disenchanted with feminists and seemed unlikely to make any more referrals to feminist therapists. During the interview, he said he had learned that (some?) feminist therapists were working out their own problems through their clients.

> I had been seeing two Native women for a bit, and I suggested they see this other therapist. They came back to me and they said, "We had to terminate with that person because she was still working out her [own] abuse issues with us. She was spending her time in therapy dealing with her anger at men; dealing with her own childhood issues, which had never been resolved; her own abuse; her own losses."I found that quite profound, because it seemed to me those women were highly sensitive to something that was happening to them. They were powerful enough to say, "We don't want this, thank you." They were able to discern that this was happening and to walk away from it.
>
> I am very fearful that there are therapists who are, under the name of empowerment, basically saying, "Here is my script for you. I am a feminist therapist. You take this script, and this is how things will work out for you." And when it comes down to the reality of the situation, the patient is not helped because they are trying to live somebody else's script, and it doesn't work. (T[64])

The differences between these two psychologists were apparent in virtually every aspect of therapy. Take fees, for instance. Both saw payment for therapy as a treatment issue, not just an economic one. But they differed in what sort of a treatment issue it was. For the male therapist, when people pay for their therapy they demonstrate their motivation:

> If they are paying out of their own pocket, they tend to be motivated quite highly. They tend to know what they want and what they don't want and tend not to stick around if you are not meeting their needs.
>
> What I say to people in the first interview is, "Consider this interview somewhat like you're a good consumer going out to buy something like an automobile. You kick the tires and bang the doors and try the lights and sound the horn. And if, at the end of the session, you feel that this is a vehicle that is going to help you get where you need to go, then you buy into it. If you think it isn't, it won't offend me any." (T[64])

The female therapist also talked to us about fee setting. She used it in therapy as an opportunity to introduce her feminist beliefs:

> We negotiate a fee. I put that in the context of feminism: Part of being a feminist is the commitment that people should have choices in all areas of their life, including therapy. If people come into therapy, it is usually because they have some difficulties to work out. I don't want the cost of therapy to add to those difficulties. So, "Without prying into your financial situation, let's figure out what you would be comfortable paying." (T[63])

Both therapists had something of a take-it-or-leave it attitude from the first session. The female psychologist told us that she introduces her feminist orientation with: "I will tell you what that means to me, and if you don't want to find out any more about that, perhaps you should go somewhere else." The male psychologist's approach was one of hard-headed consumerism: "If, at the end of the session, you feel that this is a vehicle that is going to help you get where you need to go, then you buy into it." While these sound like attempts to give the client control, we might wonder how well clients cope with either of these approaches at the outset of therapy. In telling someone who is skeptical of a feminist approach to go somewhere else, or in telling a client to kick the tires and decide whether the car will take him where he or she wants to go, the therapist has not offered any treatment options. Nor has the therapist suggested alternative ways of seeing the problem. The choice is this therapy or nothing.

These two psychologists agreed that care must be taken in treating clients who may have suffered childhood sexual abuse, but they were concerned about different problems. For the female psychologist, these patients require careful handling because their repressed memories cause them to dissociate. Dissociation into discrete personalities poses problems for informed consent.

> If someone already dissociates, which many of our clients who have repressed memories do, and we start talking in disturbing ways to them and then ask permission to do something, well, is that informed consent? Or have they already begun to dissociate when you start talking about very painful topics? We have to be really tuned in to their ways of communicating. (T[63])

The male psychologist, on the other hand, was more worried about the creation of false memories.

> There are too many therapists working out their own issues and they're harming patients and are doing a great disservice to the field of psychology. They are seeing one or two symptoms and quickly saying, "Yes, yes. That's it. Let's go for it!" And the poor patient is sort of wandering around bewildered, thinking, "If this professional person says that this happened, it must be so." And the next thing you know, you have a case developing. And you have retrieved memories and you have all sorts of other things that may or may not be accurate—they may be partially accurate. The degree of accuracy, as we all know, is highly questionable in terms of memory and recall in psychology. Look at all the research that has been done on victim identification. (T[64])

The theme of recovered memories versus false memory syndrome is important in the next section of this chapter. Turning to underlying factors, we will see that there is a major controversy about the reality of memories of early sexual abuse. The sort of treatment the client gets depends, in part, on where the therapist stands on this issue.

Discussing the Underlying Problem

Therapists are likely to fall into one of two camps with regard to the underlying factors in reports of childhood sexual abuse. One camp believes in the necessity of retrieving repressed memories of abuse; the other worries about false-memory syndrome, in which the therapist's probing creates "memories" of events that never took place. The therapist's view of this controversy plays a role in the success or failure of discussions about underlying factors.

The literature contains some famous accounts of therapy that went wrong when therapist and client had different ideas about the validity of a sexual abuse narrative. One such case is that of Henry Goddard, a major figure in American psychology, who treated a young woman with multiple personality disorder. As Ian Hacking (1991) reports the case, the client traced current problems to childhood sexual abuse, but Goddard thought the apparent memories of abuse must be a product of the child's fantasy.

Despite evidence that her dissociation was a reaction to being viciously raped by her father when she was fourteen years old, a story that her various personalities all told him under hypnosis, Goddard insisted that her story was what he called *hallucinosis incestus patris*. His evidence: Fathers simply did not do that sort of thing. The patient moved from Goddard's care at the age of twenty-two and spent the rest of her life in an asylum.

In its current form, the debate has engaged the considerable reputations of Jennifer Freyd and Elizabeth Loftus. Freyd is on the side of those who believe that child sexual abuse is often repressed and that it must be brought to the surface if treatment is to be successful. Loftus, on the other hand, is allied with those who are concerned about creating false memories. I outline their two positions as examples of prominent views that might influence the discussion of underlying factors in therapy with sexual abuse survivors.

Freyd (1994, 1996) has developed a theory of *betrayal trauma* to explain the mechanisms that underlie forgetting of early abuse, especially when perpetrated by a caregiver. She believes that forgetting becomes an adaptive response. We all have attachment needs, especially as vulnerable children. If the betrayer, such as an abusing parent, is both a potential threat and a needed object of attachment, we have to find some way to continue interacting with that person in spite of the betrayal: "It is especially crucial that a betrayed child not stop behaving in a way that will inspire attachment by parents or caregivers" (1994, pp. 317–318). In her theory, amnesia can result either while an event is being processed or after the event is fully encoded and a memory is successfully stored.

Loftus (1993, 1994) has a much different view. She has serious doubts about the sorts of amnesia that blot out whole chunks of life, only to be replaced later by vivid memories. Memory does not work that way, she says. Memories tend to fade; unless the person occasionally thinks about an event, the strength of a memory trace decreases over time. She points out that the sorts of recovered memories claimed by some alleged abuse survivors do not show this fading quality.

It is beyond the scope of this book to analyze these competing arguments. For a look at both sides, I recommend *Betrayal Trauma: The Logic of Forgetting Childhood Abuse*, by Freyd (1996), and *The Myth of Repressed Memories*, by Loftus and Ketcham (1994). For a balanced overview of the whole matter, including warnings for therapists about legal and ethical ramifications, you might refer to *Treating Patients with Memories of Abuse: Legal Risk Management,* by Knapp and Vandecreek (1997), and *Rewriting the Soul* by Ian Hacking (1995).

The question most relevant to the present study is how the divergent positions of Freyd and Loftus (and their many adherents) affect psychotherapy. Freyd has proposed the concept of *shareability* to explain how repressed memories can be recovered in the context of a therapeutic relationship. Even though there has been apparently complete repression of a memory, there may be a shareable trace laid down for future communication. Through the process of sharing we recode internal material. As the information is prepared for communication, it also becomes available to our own conscious awareness.

Loftus believes memory retrieval can be iatrogenic; what seems to be retrieved may actually be created. Why would therapists use suggestion that might lead a person to develop a false memory of child molestation? Loftus believes that the therapist adopts a theory of early abuse as an available or convenient explanation for a variety of symptoms that have not been previously explainable to either the therapist or the client. In some cases, according to Loftus and Ketcham (1994), patients with suggestive symptom profiles have been informed by their therapist, after a single consultation, that they were undoubtedly victims of abuse.

We found therapists on both sides of the fence. Some believed that one must help the client to recover memories of early trauma in order to make progress with current problems. Others were more concerned about creating false memories. An elderly psychiatrist pointed out that there had been a dramatic rise in apparent prevalence of child abuse. He wondered how much was invented by suggestible clients influenced by the media.

> The populace are not only suggestible but are fantasy prone, and they believe what they are told or what they read. If somebody says in one of these sexual abuse handbooks, "If you have mood swings and you at times feel down in the dumps, you probably were sexually abused," then they will come to believe they were. They will then begin to fantasize and imagine and then lose contact. Was that fantasy or was that reality? That's quite a serious problem, people who invent and sometimes believe their own inventions about sexual abuse. (T[23])

Many therapists take both positions into account when treating clients who may or may not have been sexually abused. They want to validate the client's reported experience, including recovered memories of early trauma, while not making suggestions that lead clients to create memories of events that never occurred.

A young university professor who was a specialist in substance abuse among women had discovered that in many cases this problem was related to a history of early sexual trauma. She used a learning model to explain the connection:

> Are the women trying to dampen the memories of the abuse with alcohol? Or is it more that, in certain situations where they are reminded of the abuse, they experience arousal and use alcohol to dampen that?
>
> Some women who have experienced sexual abuse in the past, avoid future sexual activity. It makes sense [on the basis of] a learning model of fears. Alcohol may be used in those situations to allow sexual contact. It's used to deal with the avoidance of the feared situation.
>
> I became very interested in that and sought out clients that were either substance-abusing women or women who had experienced trauma. I can't think of a single case where there wasn't both things going on. (T[69])

Despite her clinical experience that substance abuse and sexual trauma are highly correlated, she was cautious about applying this model to new clients. She was worried about the possibility of creating false memories.

> Somebody comes in and she's a substance-abusing female, and every other patient you've ever seen that's been a substance abuser also had a history of sexual abuse and physical abuse or some kind of traumatic event. If you ask about that in the initial interview and they deny it, I don't think that means you continue to fish, and fish, and fish, and believe, "Well, they have repressed that memory." I think that you just keep your ears and your eyes open for the possibility that it might come up. But it is a dangerous thing to make assumptions that "the reason this person is substance abusing is because they have had this previous traumatic event, and, if they don't think they have, I'm going to convince them in therapy." That leads to the whole false memory experience. (T[69])

The problem is, How does one guard against the possibility of false memories while still being accepting of the stories of the past that the client brings to therapy? The same therapist reflected on this issue and in the process indicated her distrust of hypnotism and the altered states it produces:

> I think the evidence is quite clear from [recent work on memory] that therapists do, inadvertently at times, encourage patients to retrieve memories, and that it is very difficult to know if they are real memories. My way of dealing with that is always to ask in the beginning, with the initial interview, using careful wording, you know, "Has anyone touched you in a way that was uncomfortable for you?" Just allowing that possibility to come up, and not asking leading questions when it does come up. Just allowing them to talk if they want to talk about it.
>
> If there is a history of any abuse, therapy works to help people through exposure to difficult memories. They are very traumatic memories, and so they try to push them out of their head. That is why they often have intrusive thoughts—they haven't fully processed [past events] emotionally. In therapy, they have a chance to discuss it and to expose themselves to the memory. (T[69])

This is an interesting combination of the positions of Freyd and Loftus. The therapist believes, with Freyd, that clients who have suffered traumatic experiences often repress them without complete processing. In the act of discussing this early history of abuse with a therapist, the client is able to remember the events and deal with them. But, with Loftus, she also believes that it is possible to influence the client to remember things that never happened. She is cautious in her approach so that she does not suggest to the client what ought to be remembered. At the same time, she feels that if a therapist worries too much about false-memory syndrome, the client's actual experience may be devalued:

> I find it a difficult situation—and I think it's difficult for the client—where there has truly been abuse but you err on the side of believing that most of the cases out there are false memory syndrome. [Because of that belief] you hold this incredible skepticism about any time a patient brings up a memory of sexual abuse or physical abuse. The biggest danger is that this person's experience isn't being validated.
>
> It is better to err on the side of what the client is presenting to you. [You should be] willing to talk about these previous experiences, validate them when the person first brings them up, make them feel like it is an environ-

ment where they are comfortable to talk about that. But at the same time, to balance that with skepticism, knowing that sometimes they are searching for a reason for the way that they are today.

So you have to maintain that [skepticism], but you keep it to yourself. You don't present it to the client. That attitude will prevent you from asking leading questions that make somebody go on to [creating] a memory—or adding details to a memory that may not be valid. (T[69])

We can see how this approach, balanced though it may be, limits negotiation with the client. The therapist retains a certain skepticism about recovered memories but does not share this skepticism with this client for fear of invalidating the experiences the client brings to therapy.

Some of the same issues, including the tension between accepting the client's lived experience and falling into the false-memory trap, were on the minds of other therapists who dealt with abuse survivors. Earlier in this chapter I presented the negotiating style of a constructivist psychologist with a hospital-based practice. She, too, tried to steer between creating false memories and the danger of rejecting clients' reports of memories of abuse.

My concern about false-memory syndrome is that some people who are truly victims of abuse may have their memories dismissed when in fact they are true. Sometimes, in cases I'm aware of, the therapist has jumped to conclusions [and] planted a seed. I can think of a few situations where I have been very cautious with patients. They have come in and said, "My siblings were all abused by so-and-so I must have been too, but I am not remembering it."

One has to be very sensitive to that situation, because what is this individual telling you? They don't have any memories, but older and younger siblings have spoken to them about abuse. They are wondering why they weren't abused or whether they have blocked and dissociated so effectively that they can't remember. There hasn't been any evidence that the individual could come up with that he or she was in fact abused.

False-memory syndrome is something that is worthwhile to look at and explore, but I am very concerned about it ending up hurting people who have truly been victimized and truly traumatized and then society groups them, saying, "You made this all up," when it may not be the case. (T[60])

Both of the therapists I have just presented wrestle with the problem of keeping a healthy skepticism about possible false memories, while trying not to invalidate the client's reported experience.

What is the client's perception of this difficulty? We talked about that issue with a mother of two who had been sexually abused and was later treated for severe bulimia. Her abuse perpetrators were two teenaged neighbors, one of whom hanged himself in his garage.

This client had been in therapy with two of the therapists in our study. One therapist was a male psychoanalytically trained psychiatrist, and the other was a female behavioral psychologist. Both therapists were true to their orientations. The psychiatrist believed that the roots of problems such as eating disorders lay in the past and was eager to explore the client's childhood for clues to present problems. The psychologist, on the other hand, kept the focus of therapy the present and future goals. But the client felt a strong need to understand the origins of her problem, and she resented the refusal of the cognitive-behavioral therapist to explore the past.

> She wanted to look to the future. I wanted to deal with my past. Things that I felt were the reason—I don't know whether they *were* the reason or not, but I wanted to deal with some of those issues. She wanted nothing to do with the past. It was more, "Look to the future, forget the past." And I just couldn't. (C[22])

When the client insisted that the therapist talk with her about the sexual abuse she suffered at the hands of her two neighbors, she claimed the therapist was dismissive:

> She said, "You must have been very pretty as a young girl 'cause guys don't get erections for no reason at all." That's when I decided to leave her. I walked out, and I never went back to her. (C[22])

In this chapter we have seen cases in which clients wanted to deal with a current problem, such as an eating disorder, and to leave the past alone. And we have seen cases in which the client felt a strong need to look for the origins of the problem. This seems to be fertile ground for negotiation between therapist and client, but, as we know, that negotiation is sometimes neglected. The outcome can be disastrous for the therapeutic relationship.

Dissociation

Many therapists who specialize in clients who suffered early sexual abuse find that some of those clients also display dissociative states, including full-blown multiple personalities. Dissociative symptoms, however, are not a sure sign of early sexual abuse. As a female psychologist told us:

> There is no particular diagnostic label per se that fits all survivors. It is important to recognize that the range of problems people can display after having been exposed to situations of abuse at very young ages is quite wide. Dissociative features can be characteristic of a lot of other current problems including posttraumatic stress disorder. (T[60])

Therapists who find themselves working with one client who seems at times to be various clients, or "alters," have special problems in negotiating consent. Some of these alters are supposed to be unknown to the actual person who came for therapy. With whom, then, does one negotiate consent? A psychologist who specialized in hypnotism with dissociative patients reflected on this problem.

> What actually constitutes informed consent? I have a consent form that I use for psychological procedures. What do you do, have all the alters sign one? What I always try to do with patients, multiple or not, is obtain a consent in the sense that I have explained myself to the patient well enough, and I have said to them, "Do you understand what we are talking about? Give me back a little bit of that so I know. And will this be all right with you?"
>
> I can think of times when I haven't recognized that the patient was in as much distress upon leaving because the patient looked okay. And yet the patient comes in the next session and says, "Gee, I really felt spaced out, and I felt like I was in a kind of a cloud for awhile." What has happened is the switch has taken place. A couple of alters have moved in, taken over, and done what they have always done for her at that point—helped her—and so she looked perfectly fine on the outside.
>
> That is the type of thing you negotiate in therapy: "If that continues, be sure to call me, and we will just talk on the phone and we will work it out." But it is always a concern. (T[64])

In addition to informed consent, therapists who work with dissociative patients may have awkward problems with confidentiality. Should the therapist keep what one alter says confidential from other alters? We interviewed an occupational therapist in private practice who had a master's degree in adult education. She believed in free communication within the system—that is, among the various alters. She told us she dealt with the confidentiality issue by discouraging secrets.

> There has only been one instance where I have not told other people in the system what has gone on between me and one alter. Bobby is a twelve-year-old male alter in a forty-four-year-old woman. He is going through all of the standard adolescent identity crises that any twelve-year-old should go through. Plus, he is feeling very upset that he is a boy in a woman's body, so that even if he grows up he can't have what he would consider a normal sex life. And he has all kinds of questions and major misconceptions about sex, like any adolescent.
>
> The main thing was that he didn't want the other alters to know about it, because it was sort of twelve-year-old boy stuff. I felt that that was perfectly appropriate and there was no need for the other alters or the host personality to know. I said, "Sure, it's not a problem." But, generally speaking, I don't think it is good to do that.
>
> There are some really interesting ethical issues that arise. The bottom line is that we can't play God. We can't really hide information from people, and, at the same time, we can't force them to hear things that they are not ready to hear. So it's kind of a juggling act. (T[57])

Another therapist we interviewed also had concerns about informed consent and confidentiality in dissociative patients. She started her career as a nurse, then worked as a psychiatric nurse, and finally returned to school and became a clinical psychologist. At the time of the interview, she had had a number of dissociative patients, and she often used hypnosis to facilitate communication between alters. She told us that no matter how real the therapist takes the various personalities to be, for purposes of informed consent, "You have to remember that you are dealing with one person, not multiple people." But on the issue of confidentiality, she said she treats the alters as though they were different people, and she is willing to maintain confidentiality between them and the host person.

> Even doing hypnosis with a normal person, there may be information that they give up at an unconscious level that they don't have conscious awareness of. It is *their* memory, not *your* memory. The dutiful therapist would always leave suggestions for [the client] to remember what is necessary for

healing. I would not necessarily tell the host, because different parts of different alters can have information that they believe from their perspective is true, but it may not necessarily be true. So what you do is you listen, and in time that information is going to filter through as the patient improves and the barriers between the different unconscious states come down. That information can be shared and then checked if [the client] chooses, for verification. (T[58])

According to this account, it is the therapist who makes the decisions about what to keep hidden from the host personality and whether to leave clues during hypnosis. Clearly, the combination of doing hypnosis and dealing with dissociative states restricts the room for negotiation between therapist and client.

Therapists differ in their belief in multiple personality and its prevalence in the client population. There are also some therapists who believe that there is a choice about whether to work with a client as a multiple personality. They believe that, to some extent, the therapist makes that choice. The therapist I just quoted reflected on the possibility that the therapist "creates" alters by using a particular treatment approach. Here is her view of the matter:

Of the five multiples that I now have on my caseload, only one came to me with that diagnosis. The others came with depression and inability to cope, anxiety disorders, things like that. I've had some who, when I tell them what Multiple Personality Disorder is, say, "Oh, yeah!" Or the husband says, "Yeah, that's so-and-so," referring to different parts that they have already labeled, like "the bitch." So then it makes sense to them.

I have had one gal who didn't want the term used. Another patient that I have worked with for quite a long time—a male—is at the point where he is trying to decide, and I have left this with him, whether or not he wants to approach therapy as an MPD. He certainly *has* MPD, but we have been dealing with the issues individually and not looking at the whole system. And his system is very defensive. One of the personalities came forward for the first time and said that she didn't want anyone in her world. So I said we'd respect that. We're not going to charge in. So we just talked about the disorder. I have a video on MPD. And so I sat with him and watched that and let him go away and decide.

With others I don't know if it [being treated for dissociation] has been helpful or not. I would have to ask the question. I, too, have seen it from the videos: "Whew, it's wonderful to hear this." But my experience is, it hasn't been wonderful for *them* to hear it. (T[58])

This is a very frank comment about the influence therapists may have over how clients present themselves and their problems in psychotherapy. Just as some therapists fear creating false memories, this therapist wonders about the wisdom of encouraging personality splits.

As usual, opinion is divided about dissociative states. Some tie dissociation firmly to early childhood trauma, others point out that adult trauma can be followed by dissociation, and still others think the therapist has a lot to do with the emergence of dissociative phenomena. We did not find consensus even on the question of whether multiple personalities are born or made. A young male psychiatrist working in public health believed that some people have a predisposition to dissociate:

> The ability to dissociate is almost like an innate property of certain people, and those that utilize it and then go on to develop dissociative disorders have that propensity from an early age, as opposed to those that develop say post-traumatic stress disorder or something like that without dissociative elements. (T[59])

This notion of a possible predisposition to react to problems in a certain way came up in several interviews. The head of a psychological service department, for example, reflected on why people differ so much in their ability to cope with difficult circumstances, including abuse. She had seen such different reactions among people who seemed to have similar histories that she, too, considered possible predisposition.

> You have to wonder, why did person X, who was terribly abused, manage to go through till age thirty without an inpatient admission despite having a hard life and flashbacks and problems, while person Y, with a similar history, was admitted to inpatient units since early adolescence. They could have a similar history and a very dissimilar pattern of functioning.
>
> I would like to tease out what it is that makes a person able to go through the motions of a reasonable life, whereas another person cannot. It doesn't seem to be the extent of the abuse. So maybe it's an inherited temperament or strength. It could be that somehow they were structurally weaker as people. (T[68])

Although therapists who wondered about "structural weaknesses" talked to us about them, they did not share these views with their clients. In this important area, then, the therapist and client were not discussing what the therapist considered a possible underlying factor. Why not? Perhaps because they did not feel there was enough evidence upon which to base a devastating opinion. Or perhaps, like the therapist with whom I ended the chapter 4, they were unwilling to undercut the client's hope.

Summary

Control is generally thought to be an important issue in therapy with survivors of sexual abuse. The client is perceived to have been victimized and to need as much control as possible in the therapeutic situation. Symbolic of this approach is the tendency to refer to abuse victims as survivors, a small gesture but one that fits the theme of empowerment. In this area, the ongoing negotiation of consent throughout therapy is not only an ethical issue but an essential component of treatment. As one therapist said in a trenchant comment, "Being forced to touch your uncle's penis or being forced to tell a therapist about doing it—in both cases, you are being forced."

Given this emphasis on control, it is somewhat paradoxical that the one treatment traditionally associated with this problem area is hypnosis and that a characteristic symptom is dissociation. Classical hypnosis does not seem to be the sort of treatment relationship that would encourage client control. Nevertheless there is increasing integration of some hypnotic techniques with approaches such as feminist therapy, where therapists claim that it can be used in ways that heighten client control of the process.

Dissociation, especially in cases where discrete personalities emerge in therapy, gives a bizarre twist to standard ethical procedures. We heard from therapists who wondered which personality should give consent and whether consent from one personality can be taken as consent for all. Other therapists were concerned about confidentiality—not the usual question of whether to guard the confidence of a client, but whether to tell one personality what was said by another in the same body.

Therapists and clients who were interviewed for this chapter talked about some other problems associated with treatment of survivors, including the sex of the therapist, whether to encourage the client to file a legal report about the offender, and the issue of which problem should take priority, the problem brought to therapy by the client or the history of sexual abuse that may underlie the current problem.

For therapists who want to deal with a history of abuse, there remains the question of how much the client remembers. Some therapists see their primary task as helping the client to recover repressed memories and then to deal with them. Others worry that these memories are not so much recovered as created in the therapeutic process. The controversy over the accuracy of recovered memories was well known to the therapists we interviewed. Some took sides, but others tried to steer between the shoals, neither suggesting memories of abuse nor invalidating the client's account of such trauma.

In choosing to focus on three problem domains for this book, I assumed that negotiating consent might pose different challenges according to the sort of problem being treated. Looking at two of the domains, eating disorders and sexual abuse, we have seen that this is true. There are more specific treatments for eating disorders, but somewhat less negotiation. There are fewer discrete treatments for the aftermath of sexual abuse, but therapists put more emphasis on client control of the healing process. In chapter 6 we will see another spin on consent when the clients are sex offenders who may be under court order to attend therapy.

6

■ ■ ■ ■ ■ ■ ■ ■

Sex Offenders

NOW WE TURN from survivors of abuse to sex offenders. In doing so, we move into a treatment area in which room for negotiating consent, or anything else, is extremely limited. Most therapists who deal with offenders work within a framework established by the legal system. That framework puts serious limits on the freedom of the adult offender to select type of treatment, type of therapist, and so on.

I begin with a portrait of an offender, using his own words. We interviewed two clients for this chapter, referred to by the pseudonyms Jake and Morgan. Jake was an incest offender who abused young girls in his family, including his daughter and his granddaughters. Morgan was a younger married man who abused a young boy.

The opening sketch is of Jake, who embodies many of the difficulties that therapists talk about later in the chapter. His daughter did not independently report his abuse of her. Some years later he abused his granddaughters, and charges were laid when the children's mother, Jake's daughter-in-law, found out. At that point his daughter, now an adult, also came forward. Jake was convicted of several offenses and, in addition to serving some jail time, had to undergo treatment. While Jake reported socially appropriate remorse (he said he had learned in therapy that he had a "kind of a sickness"), he did not agree that charges should have been filed against him.

> I would have preferred that they had done it some other way, rather than have in the authorities. I mean, they all knew: my wife, and my son, and everybody else knew that I was trying to straighten out my life. I think it would have been a lot easier for everybody all the way around. Now I am not saying this because I feel that it would help people stay out of jail. I am not saying it for that reason. But I think it could have been resolved by having family sessions or by going through somebody: maybe a psychiatrist, a psychologist, family services, or whatever. (C[92])

Jake is obviously defensive, but, as we will see when discussing treatment alternatives, there is a body of opinion that suggests that incest offenders like him may in fact be best suited to what Jake called "family sessions." But often the family is not interested in working with offenders like Jake in therapy—or in seeing them at all. Family members often take out restraining orders against the offender that limit the possibility of a family approach, as his daughter-in-law had done in Jake's case.

Although some believe that family therapy is an appropriate treatment for the incest offender, they still believe offenders should be charged. That is not Jake's view. His high level of defensiveness, which would pose major problems for therapists, is evident in the "therapeutic" tone he adopts when talking about his effort to keep one of the abuse victims quiet:

> In one case, my youngest granddaughter, I hadn't abused her for over two years. Matter of fact, I told her what I was doing was wrong and that it would stop, because that was when I started to get healed myself. So she really knew, I think, a lot more than what other victims did, because I had told her that what I was doing was wrong, that I would go to jail if she had to reveal it. All I did was ask her, if it was possible, to keep it to herself and forget it. I sat down and told her all of that. (C[92])

The manipulation that therapists must contend with is evident in Jake's description of how he tried to get his granddaughter not to report him. Jake is far from taking responsibility for his problems. Like many sex offenders, he blames the person who brought the charges—in this case, his daughter-in-law. He talked with approval about his daughter, who kept his secret for years. He compared her unfavorably with his daughter-in-law, whom he saw as the real cause of the problem.

> When my mother died, my daughter and I sort of got together by fate or by reason of my mother's death. I talked to my daughter about it, and we resolved everything. And there is never any mention about it since. Everything is fine as far as my daughter is personally concerned. The big problem at the present time in my situation is my daughter-in-law, which I don't believe will ever be resolved. She will be this way the rest of her life. She is that type of a person, anyway. (C[92])

The challenge for a therapist is how to get through the offender's way of structuring a world in which the victim, or the person reporting the offense, is really to blame. The legal system plays an important role in most treatment programs. It gets offenders into treatment even though they are in denial or are extremely defensive and manipulative. Of course, as it reduces the offender's room to maneuver, it also limits negotiation between therapist and client. For that reason, as we turn to this population, we will see less of the sort of negotiation that has been discussed in previous chapters.

Even so, there are areas in which discussion does take place, and where therapists have different views about the amount of choice that should be available to the offender.

Negotiating Consent

In this section I cover the general relationship between legal proceedings and treatment, then consider whether, in this treatment context, offenders are "clients" at all.

Most therapists see the legal process as an important aspect of therapy with sex offenders, especially when those offenders are adults. We interviewed a psychologist who, after completing his doctorate, made a career of working with sex offenders. Like many other therapists in this domain, he tended to work with offenders in a structured group program. He outlined the legal context of treatment:

> We want to have absolute control over these individuals. We won't take any offender into the group until all of the legal aspects of the case have been resolved. He has either pleaded guilty or he has been convicted. And, if he has

pleaded guilty or been convicted, he has been sentenced. We put the further stipulation that that sentence would have to include some kind of condition or clause that mandated treatment as part of the punishment. What that means is: If you decide you are going to come to the groups but not partic- ipate, merely fulfill the condition that you had to take the treatment, it gives us the opportunity to say, "We will judge you as a treatment failure. We will turn around and report that back to the referring probation officer or parole officer who could go back to court and say you are not complying with the condition." We want to make sure that if the program is going to run fifteen weeks, we see them for fifteen weeks. (T^{55})

We heard a similar view of the interaction between law and therapy from separate interviews we conducted with a male-female pair of cotherapists who work with groups of adult sex offenders. The male is a psychologist, and the female is a social worker. The social worker was the main formal connection between the team and the legal system. She had worked as a probation and parole officer, and for the five years preceding the interview she had worked primarily with sex offenders. She described the formal structure for treatment of adult offenders in their group:

When I write my report, I ask for conditions on their probation order. These conditions include that the person participate in counseling for issues of anger management, marital counseling, financial counseling, and so on. So that way the person no longer has the decision or choice in whether to par- ticipate. The court is telling them, "You do as the probation officer tells you to." So we have some clout with that individual. (T^{85})

Clearly, this framework restricts negotiation in ways we would not find in treating persons with eating disorders or in therapy with survivors of sexual abuse.

Negotiation is limited not only by legal constraints but also by how therapists see the personal characteristics of the usual sex offenders: They are seen as defensive, often in denial, and generally manipulative. It is to cut through manipulation that therapists welcome the rules imposed by the courts.

The need to confront manipulation has led to increasing emphasis on groups, rather than on individual treatment. The psychologist I quoted earlier, who said therapists wanted to have "absolute control" over of- fenders, described this aspect of group work:

One of the big things in the treatment with these individuals is the initial aspect of denial. Even if they are convicted, they often will explain to you that it has been a miscarriage of justice—that the victim committed perjury.

I think why group therapy works better than individual therapy is the need for confrontation. We end up with [charge] sheets on every one of our offenders. So we know exactly, at least from the prosecutor's viewpoint, what was involved in the assault, how it took place, when it took place, and so on. And if Johnny Jones is going to say these things aren't true, then we confront him with the sheet and we say, "Okay, you explain this, explain that, explain the other thing."

We may spend the first third of the fifteen-week program focusing just on the act itself—going over it and over it. "Tell us again what happened? Tell us, again, why you think you got convicted if in fact it didn't happen?" We will confront them in terms of their credibility. It can get to be pretty confrontational—much more so than is likely in individual therapy. (T[55])

The problem of denial of responsibility fits the case of Jake, with which I began this chapter. You will recall that he laid the blame for his ensuing problems not on what he had done (he was "healing himself," after all) but on his vindictive daughter-in-law, who insisted on laying charges.

The male-female team also believes firmly in group therapy. The cotherapists told us that other group members are crucial in identifying and cutting through defensiveness and denial. The psychologist member of the pair had worked in corrections for fifteen years, during which he had been involved with developing and delivering several types of treatment programs. His experience included community residential centers (halfway houses) for men being released from prison. He had worked in minimum-, medium-, maximum-, and what are called supermaximum security prisons. He had worked in an institution especially designed for what the law still calls the criminally insane. Here was his argument for group treatment:

You should never do a treatment program with sex offenders on an individual basis only. They are used to manipulating. They like secrets. They are good at it. They have developed it over many years. So dealing with somebody one on one is like playing a game of chess. They've got the secrets, and they will determine when they are going to give them up and if they are going to give them up.

In a group they are being badgered; other people are not giving them any space. Gee, it sounds like a battle, and a few minutes ago I was calling them clients! (T[94])

This therapist spontaneously raised the question of whether people seen under these conditions are really clients. His sudden doubt about the status of sex offenders in therapy came after he had been defending the view that they are clients—because if the therapist did not see them as such, it would be hard to work with them.

They are very much clients that you work with. If you look at them as "offenders," then it is difficult to build a therapeutic relationship with them. It is difficult to gain their confidence or trust. And with sex offenders, perhaps more so than other types of populations, there is a lot of disclosing that has to be done. There is a lot of denial, minimizing, projecting—because of the nature of the crime. It is shameful in our society, and a lot of them actually feel bad about doing it. So the term "client" is appropriate. (T[94])

The notion of client may be employed here to give the therapist a rationale for what might otherwise seem coercive treatment. It is also used, apparently, to help the therapist relate to someone who has done horrifying crimes. The difficulty of building rapport in light of the client's distasteful crimes was brought up in our interview with another co-therapist pair. This team comprised two men, a psychologist and a pastoral counselor. As the pastoral counselor put it:

There are times when the awareness of the event—I found it taxed me powerfully. I just had to sit back for a second and think, "My God, he did this to that child, and what a horrible thing." But it's really important not to have that come out in therapy. [What they have done] has unquestionably marred and wounded another individual. But these are still human beings. (T[39])

It may be therapeutic to consider the offender as a client, but it is realistic? They are typically in treatment under duress, and they have restrictions on the type of therapy they can choose and the therapists they can see. The psychologist member of the male-female pair had mulled over these ethical issues:

Whenever you are dealing with an offender population, you have the ethical issue of: Who are you providing treatment for? Are you providing it for your employer, which happens to be the government? Or some agency like the John Howard Society? Is it for the offender himself? Or is it for the protection of society? Oh, and the victims. It may be an incest case where you still have that ongoing dynamic of the relative—the mother or the daughter or whoever. You really have different people or populations that you are working for and so you have to have everything balanced in your mind. (T[94])

If everything the sex offender said, asked, or demanded were chalked up to manipulation, there would be no room for negotiation at all. But the picture is not as stark as it seems. There are various examples of possible negotiation between sex offenders and therapist. For example, if a sex offender has difficulty with a particular therapist, it is often taken seriously. The cotherapist pair said such an issue, raised by an offender, prompts serious consultation within the treatment team. Something about the offender has touched a nerve in the therapist, who is showing prejudice that makes it difficult to work with that individual. The psychologist described the problem:

> When you are working with somebody, there is always a possibility that you may become biased or jaded. And so you bounce it off your colleagues to make sure what's going on here. (T[94])

It is clear, both from our study and from a review of the literature (see Wormith and Hansen, 1992), that the current trend is to treat sex offenders under legal warrant and in packaged groups. The psychologist with a career in the penal system said that any latitude permitted in such group programs is latitude for a group, because *groups* differ, not for individual differences:

> There really is a definite syllabus, if I can use that word, to define what we include in the program. There are certain points that we definitely want to cover. But then there is a lot of latitude and flexibility if the group, for whatever reason, seems to need more emphasis in part X than they do in part Y, then we just adjust it for that particular group. (T[55])

Individuals do differ, of course, and there is increasing concern about whether one-size-fits-all groups can help everyone. For example, how does one integrate into such a program people who have weak verbal skills, either because English is not their primary language or because of low intelligence or poor education? Even a staunch defender of group treatment, the psychologist in our male-female pair, was concerned about the inability of programmed groups to meet the needs of such people.

> You have a lot of immigrants—a lot of refugees who know very little English. We don't have a lot of services for them. Or you may have a lower-functioning fellow that comes into the system, and he has done a sexual crime. He would probably think that he didn't do that much that was that wrong. And unless he gets a lot of treatment and attention, he will probably go out and do it again, because he doesn't know specifically what he did wrong. However, most of our programs are for average-level, eighth-grade, tenth-grade reading abilities. And they have treatment manuals and exercises geared for that. That's it, period.
>
> So we try to do the greatest good for the greatest number with the funds we have. But a lot of people are likely to reoffend if they receive a lower quality of treatment or receive very little treatment at all.
>
> If you had extra treatment dollars floating around it might be nice to try to direct them towards some of those at higher risk to reoffend, the people that don't get access to treatment: lower functioning, foreign speaking. (T[94])

Legal Charges

So far, I have presented a picture of therapy that requires interaction between treatment and the justice system. In a moment, I will turn to therapy outside the legal system. But first, let's consider the question of legal charges. Generally, therapists agree that charges ought to be laid, while clients are, understandably, less convinced. We heard Jake's rationale for dealing with his problems outside the legal system. The social worker member of our male-female pair of cotherapists had no doubt about the necessity of laying charges. She gave an example of what happens when charges are not laid:

> A fellow recently was referred; he has a lot of power, a lot of authority. He is a successful businessman. Both of his daughters had been abused by him. One of them told him, "I want you to go get help. I am not going to press criminal charges or go to the police or anything but I want you to get help." So the guy comes in, and I see him, and he is very resistant. He is not there because he thinks he needs help; he is there because he sees himself as being blackmailed to being there.

I really think that there needs to be that confronting of the denial and having the person appear in court and go through that. There has to be some legal involvement and court-mandated treatment, and if the person doesn't [do what the court requires], then there needs to be consequences for that. Bring them back to court, have them sentenced. We really need that. (T[85])

If this sounds as though treatment is more part of the punishment than anything like the therapies presented in earlier chapters, the therapists do not see it that way. One rationale is that the legal system provides the motivation for treatment: It gets offenders into the room. But over time, that motivation can be converted to reasons less based on fear. The social worker cotherapist described the process:

They don't want to be in jail again, to have to go before the court, to face that publicity around another offense. I don't want them to hurt any more kids. I think initially our goals are different, but they become closer. They start out initially saying, "I don't want to be in jail, and I don't want to deal with this." and then it moves more into, "I don't want to hurt anybody else." But that is a process, and it comes over time. (T[85])

Not all therapists take a hard line on the need to report abuse, even when dealing with court-referred sex offenders. The psychologist-and-pastoral-counselor pair actually cue group members about how to talk in general terms so that the therapists will not be obliged to report any disclosures they make in group. The psychologist said:

When they are in the group, we cover the confidentiality thing by telling them that, if they reveal anything else, we're obligated to report. But if they reveal it in such a way that we don't have enough information [we cannot report]. We would probably meet with them individually and try to encourage them to report themselves and deal with them that way. But as long they did not give us enough details, we really couldn't report it. We could still be dealing with it, but the focus would be on what's stopping them [from reporting]. How can they be lacking the courage to go ahead and own up and accept responsibility? (T[39])

The pastoral counselor member of the pair added that, although it is essential that an offender admit to an offense, it is not necessary that he admit *all* offenses of which he is accused.

As part of being accepted for the group they have to accept some responsibility, they have to accept, "Yes, I've sexually offended. Whether or not they accept all of the offenses—they may say, "Well, you know, I did *this*, but I'm not going to confess to *that*." The bottom line is: They have to acknowledge in some way that they have sexually offended. (T[39])

Treatment outside the Legal System

Not all treatment with offenders is done in the context of the legal system, with its severe limitation on choice. One therapist, who worked for a child protection agency, did therapy with adolescents who were often abused and abusers at the same time.

She pointed out that young people who are both survivors and offenders are a population that has not had much attention. When she realized this was an underserved group, she decided to specialize in working with its members. At the time of our interview, she was recognized as a pioneer in this niche. Contrary to what we have heard about adult sex offenders, in this program the voluntary nature of participation was emphasized.

> They can't be ordered to receive treatment from us. We will not accept an order from the court. Often what happens is the child comes in under Child Protection Services. The application is presented to the child as an option for treatment. It's not seen as sort of, "Here is a way for me to avoid doing custody time."
>
> We explain to the child, "We see treatment like building a house. The foundation is accepting responsibility for what you have done. And together we will build the house, adding skills and so forth. Then you will be living in that house. That is why the court system has become involved with you at this point in time. And it is up to you." Now some of the boys come and they see me and they're interviewed and they choose not to take treatment. And that's fine. (T[79])

This therapist, like some we have seen in previous chapters, puts foremost the need to negotiate the structure of therapy.

> In terms of the child's treatment: Right from the beginning the child contracts on how they want to start working with me. "What is the issue you want to start working on?" It might not be the issue I think is most important but what they think is important is what we start on.

> They are in control in each session. We are looking at a tremendous amount of flexibility. If a boy comes in for his regular appointment with me, doesn't want to work but just wants to sit or doesn't want to do anything, I will say, "Well, you know, we can go for a coffee, but what are we going to do about your session, though? I have to earn my keep." (T[79])

Working with adolescents who have not been sentenced to treatment gives this social worker considerable latitude to discuss with her clients different ways to go about therapy.

> In the first session, I start with: "I need to get some idea on sort of where you are in terms of feelings . . . okay, you don't like to talk about them. What would be the easiest way for us to work on that? I can make up a board game; we can use painting; you can speak into a tape recorder; you can talk to me directly. What would be easiest for you?" So there is some element of control right there. "How would you like to use the session?" Some guys like to spend the first fifteen minutes asking me questions—just questions in general. And then we use the next forty-five minutes on working on therapeutic tasks that we've outlined together.
>
> Everything is choices—by "everything," I mean everything. They come in and they want to sit in the chair with the wheels on it, then they sit in the chair with the wheels on it. They come in and they want to use my pen and not theirs, that's fine.
>
> With most of the boys, as long as you offer the choice, that meets their control need. They are not backed in a corner, and they don't have to engage you in an all-out confrontation.
>
> "Do you want me to do the talking this session, or do you want to do the talking?" I know darn well. I will start talking and the next thing you know they have taken it away. But they've made the choice. (T[79])

The difference between the therapist who works with adolescents and those who work with adult offenders does not seem to be just a matter of working inside or outside the legal system. The therapist who works with adolescents seems to have a view of treatment, even with offenders, that puts choice and control in the hands of the client.

There is evidence in the research literature, however, that it is not easier to treat adolescent offenders than adults. Nor are adolescents less likely to reoffend. What we are seeing is probably a difference in therapist style rather than in the demands of the client population.

Presenting Alternatives

As I have said in earlier chapters, we have to know something about the treatments generally available for a problem before we can talk about what options might be offered to clients. Surveying the field of treatments for sex offenders, we find there are fewer options than for eating disorders, but more distinct forms of therapy than for treating survivors of sexual abuse.

More treatments are available than therapists generally use. Castration and medication are rare and unpopular. Voluntary castration has been reported to have good effects in some European countries, but there is skepticism about it in Great Britain and in North America. Among medications, phenothiazines dampen the sex drive but are effective only when actually being taken and have no long-lasting benefit. There is a similar problem with androgen-depleting agents, which decrease a male offender's testosterone. Although drive is decreased, the *direction* of the drive is not altered. If the problem is pedophilia, the object of sexual desire is still a child. Since these treatments are uncommon and did not show up as options in our interviews, I will not refer to them further. For a review, see Marshall, Laws, and Barbaree (1990).

What treatments are available? Only a few: empathy training, relapse prevention programs, and family therapy for incest offenders. Usually these are distinct treatments, although some therapists include some empathy training in relapse prevention programs.

Historically, a treatment that has come and (almost) gone is aversive conditioning. This is a form of behavior modification in which the offender is shown stimuli representing forbidden targets, such as children, and is given punishment at the same time. In the 1950s, behavioral programs such as aversion therapy and satiation were common. Now they have fallen out of favor, not because of any demonstration that they do not work but because they are perceived to be impersonal and dehumanizing. The change in the spirit of the times was reflected in, and affected by, the image of behavior modification presented in films such as *A Clockwork Orange* (1971).

As aversive conditioning fell into disrepute, and hence into disuse, some alternative was needed. Several prominent "humanistic" theories gave rise to therapies that focused on the offender's personality or interpersonal relationships. One of these theories suggested that sexual offenses are the result of low self-esteem and other personality deficits. This leads to treatment designed to shore up weak aspects of the personality. At the same time, as Wormith and Hansen have noted, "the women's movement began to have an impact on programs, as attention shifted to power, control, sex-role stereotyping, and attitudes toward women" (1992, p. 181).

Treatment for self-esteem and other personality deficits is still included in other programs, but it is rarely the sole treatment of choice, because there is no evidence that it works. It also puts the focus on the offender as victim, which is out of step with current thinking that emphasizes viewing the *victim* as the victim and the offender as someone who has done something wrong and needs to admit it and stop it.

How do we get offenders to stop it? The two major current approaches are empathy training and relapse prevention. Briefly, empathy training is based on the notion that sex offenders can learn to be empathic in general, toward their victims in particular, and also toward potential victims. Relapse prevention is based on the notion that offenders are motivated to stay out of jail, and this motivation can be used to train them to control their behavior. In a sense, the current popularity of relapse prevention comes out of some disenchantment with empathy training. I begin by looking at empathy training and follow with a discussion of relapse prevention.

Empathy Training

One question about empathy training is whether it really affects the feelings offenders have for other people or just teaches them the way to *talk* about feelings for others. In one of our interviews, a client discussed what empathy training had done for him, and in listening to his words we may get some sense of the problem. Earlier I introduced Jake, an elderly incest offender who had abused his daughter and later his granddaughters. Now I introduce the second client we interviewed, a man I will call Morgan, who is different from Jake in almost every way. He was a young married man who had abused a young boy some years before charges were laid. Despite these differences, Jake and Morgan were treated in the same group with the same method, a possible problem about which I have more to say at the end of this chapter. Morgan had three different therapists. Here he talks about what he learned from them.

Well, we didn't always agree, you know. [chuckles]. They'd listen to me, and I'd listen to them. That's what I found very positive. And when I expressed—if they didn't think it was the right way of expressing it or the right idea, they would explain to me why—why this way of thinking isn't right. It just wasn't, "Oh no, that's not right. You don't do it that way, you do it this way." They'd take the time to explain things to you. And sometimes I would say, or someone else in the group would say, "Well, that's a good idea. I never thought of that." (C[91])

This seems to be a picture of someone who has learned to talk the talk.

One technique in empathy training is to bring a survivor of abuse to speak to a group of offenders. A woman had visited Morgan's group, and he claimed that in listening to her account of the abuse she had suffered, some of his attitudes had changed. For example, he said that he and other group members believed that it was wrong to lay charges against offenders. But he said he changed his mind after listening to the survivor:

One thing that the therapy has done, it's made me appreciate what the victim goes through. We had a victim at one of our meetings. A lady came in and talked to us. Now you hear people say, "Well, this person I know is being charged for sexual assault." And everyone is saying, "Oh, it is terrible. That girl shouldn't charge him." And they're pissed off. "He's a nice guy." They are forgetting that the girl was the one who was violated, not the guy. Before I wouldn't have thought about it that way. (C[91])

Although Morgan claims that seeing and hearing this female survivor reminded him that "the girl is the one who was violated," we should remember that Morgan's abuse was against a male.

The popularity of empathy training led to development of a wide range of techniques that were supposed to help offenders see abuse from the victim's point of view and/or experience the feelings of a victim (the cognitive and emotional components of empathy are usually thought to be different). I have mentioned recruiting survivors to speak to offenders. Other methods include presenting lectures about the effect of abuse on victims, role playing, asking offenders to remember how they felt when they were victimized in some way, and having the offender write an account of the abuse from the victim's perspective and read it to the group.

A major problem with empathy training arises from the separation between so-called cognitive empathy and emotional empathy. The distinction is that one can learn the facts about what it might be like to be a victim without having any increase in empathic feeling for the person. Hilton (1993) makes a strong case that cognitive empathy, in the absence of emotional empathy, is either useless or harmful. First, cognitive empathy is not necessary for emotional empathy. Second, cognitive empathy is not sufficient for emotional empathy. The psychopath, who can be charming and manipulative but also shallow and callous, epitomizes the combination of well-developed cognitive empathy without emotional empathy. Third, it may be harmful to raise cognitive empathy among sex offenders. Some are psychopaths, and there is evidence that their offending actually increases when they have a better understanding of the pain and terror they inflict.

Some think empathy training is useful only if the offender was once abused (and thus has a well of residual empathy on which to draw). But Morgan, who claimed he learned a lot from empathy training, said himself had never been abused. Since he had been told about the possible connection between being a victim and later an abuser, he wondered why he offended:

> And my biggest problem was I wanted to know. I knew I committed the offense, but I wanted to know why. I racked my brains over it. You don't just wake up some morning and say, "Well, I'm going to go commit a sexual assault." There's a number of things that lead up to it in your life. It was a lot of little things in my life that were just sort of building up and building up, and all of a sudden it happened. I was not a victim, and this is what I couldn't understand. (C[91])

If all this seems rather hard on empathy training, I should point out that most therapists still use some form of it in a treatment package. To redress the balance, we will hear a powerful plea for empathy training by the therapist who has the final word in this chapter. Now, however, I move on to a type of treatment that is currently in vogue, one based on the self-interest of the offender, rather than on empathy with past and future victims. To introduce this approach, I again quote the client Morgan. But this time, rather than focusing on the empathy he says he learned in therapy, I offer a passage in which he describes the emotional consequences that resulted from the laying of charges:

> I was always looking over my shoulder if anyone would recognize me as a sex offender. But then you can't do that [forever]. When I first started the

group, I wouldn't go into a mall, or when I went shopping with my wife I would go in and come right back out. I just couldn't. "Someone is going to see me, the shame!"

This therapy got me out of that. "Hey, you made a mistake, a terrible mistake. You paid for it. You are getting help so you don't do it again. But you have to try to get your life back on track." Once in a while I will get those anxiety attacks [in a public place], but I stay there, you know, instead of leaving. I will finish shopping with the wife or stay in the mall with her, instead of going out and sitting in the car and waiting for her to come out, like I did just after I come home from being incarcerated.

Oh, it's a terrible feeling. I just gradually started going in with the wife maybe ten minutes at a time and then a little longer, a little longer, and if I get a little attack now I'll just ride it out. (C[91])

We may have doubted Morgan's depth of feeling about empathy training, but there is no question about his experience of being seen as a sex offender. Relapse prevention makes full use of these sorts of feelings. Therapists rely on the motivation to protect oneself from shame and harm that results from coming before the legal system.

Relapse Prevention Programs

Relapse prevention is based on a theoretical model developed by Pithers and his colleagues (Pithers et al., 1983). The basic assumption of the model is that the offender can learn to recognize risk situations and exert control over potentially harmful urges. Offenses are often the end product in a sequence of arousal, fantasy, planning, and seeking an opportunity. The earlier in this sequence that the client can exert self-control, the less likely it is that the offense will occur (Gillies, et al., 1992).

Here is one of the therapists in our study, the psychologist in the male-female cotherapist pair, describing the sequence that leads to an offense:

We dealt with a fellow a little while ago who had seen a Clint Eastwood movie—one of the *Dirty Harry* movies, in which the scene opened with a woman being gang-raped under the boardwalk. It excited him, and he went home and kept thinking about that particular scene. He took the next progression to masturbating to that fantasy. Then he took the next progression to walking around the neighborhood looking for women to be able to use in his fantasy material: women's faces, the shape of the woman, or whatever, to the point of pretend stalking. And it just escalated and escalated and ended in rape.

This therapist described the way the relapse prevention program works with such offenders. He was an expert on this approach, having practiced it, taught it, and written a book about it (he was the second book author among our therapist participants).

> The relapse prevention orientation gets at the warning cues to help clients manage them. We go in saying, "We want to know why you did your offense, the circumstances under which you decided to do your offense. What were your thoughts, feelings, behaviors before, during, and after your offense?" And through that we gain some idea of early warning signs: risky thoughts, feelings, or behaviors, persons or places that may lead the client to consider doing inappropriate sexual or deviant acts. By piecing together their stressors or precursors before their offenses, you can start to get an idea of the etiology—how they started developing inappropriate thoughts, inappropriate feelings, and inappropriate behaviors. Sometimes, once you break down the defense mechanisms you can find an individual who will tell you the beginning was at a much younger age. When he was in his teens, he started having inappropriate fantasies. (T[94])

One reason for the popularity of relapse prevention programs is the increasing belief that lack of motivation is the major barrier to treatment. Langevin, Wright, and Handy (1988) asked the question "What treatment do sex offenders want?" They found the answer is usually no treatment at all. Therapists have translated such observations into an urgent need to find out what the offender *is* motivated to do and to start from there. They find that the offender is motivated to stay out of jail.

I have spent comparatively little time in this chapter talking about the way in which therapists present options to their clients. The reason is that by and large they do not present any. Treatment packages, usually for groups, are popular. Requests for different approaches are seen as manipulation.

Is this a field, then, in which the concept of different treatments for different people is simply irrelevant? Many therapists we talked to gave us that impression, although there was an exception: the social worker who engaged in full-scale negotiation with adolescent offenders.

Despite the practice of offering a packaged program for offenders, there is a good deal of evidence that offenders differ and that these differences can and should lead to different sorts of treatment. The Canadian Psychological Association (1988), in a brief to the Government of Canada, said that treatment of sex offenders works best when there is individualized treatment planning.

Offenders and programs may be mismatched in various ways. Group programs tend to focus on management of arousal with the primary goal of prevention of reoffending. But some of the men in those groups were incest offenders whose sexual abuse was limited to their own family members. Incest offenders are generally not at high risk to reoffend, and, if they do so, it tends to be a further offense within the family. Nor do incest offenders need arousal management. They are generally better served by a family approach, such as that pioneered by Giaretto, Giaretto, and Sgroi (1978), which emphasizes working with all members of the incest family. As Wormith and Hansen put it, "Programs for treating incest offenders may reasonably involve a different set of goals and treatment procedures" (1992, p. 193).

There are important differences among incest offenders that have implications for treatment. Two major types of incest offenders have been identified by Groth and Birnbaum (1978): the fixated offender and the regressed offender. Fixated offenders are those whose primary sexual attraction is to a child; regressed offenders are oriented toward adult sexual partners. Even among the regressed offenders, there are two distinct types: the passive-dependent type, who feels inadequate with adult women and the aggressive-dominant type, who gains a sense of strength and control in a relationship with a weaker, younger female. According to Groth and Birnbaum, all these variations require different treatments and have different prognoses.

Discussing the Underlying Problem

In this section three underlying factors in sexual abuse are discussed: the way sex offenders see women, the role of drugs and alcohol in sex offenses, and the question of whether a history of being abused is a factor in becoming an abuser.

In the case of offenders whose targets were women, the way they see women provides a good example of the connection between an underlying problem and a treatment strategy. Such offenders often have difficulty relating to women as equals or as authority figures. They prefer that women not be assigned as their therapists. Treatment programs recognize this and sometimes (but not always) insist that women be included in the treatment program.

One client told us it was important for offenders to change the way they viewed women and that therapy can help accomplish this. Jake, you will recall, had a long history of abusing female children in his family. He summed up his general attitude toward women:

> You want to prove that you can get as many women as possible or something like that. I had the wrong attitude about women as a sex symbol or whatever. All I cared about was my own pleasure out of whatever I was doing. (C[92])

The male-female therapist pair we interviewed was adamant about not permitting clients to exclude the possibility of a woman therapist. The male therapist explained:

> You want to show that there is equality, that there is an appropriate way of dealing with females, that females are assertive. A lot of sex offenders have problems around females. They have stereotypical attitudes: Women are second-class citizens who are to be used for only one thing, and all this type of nonsense. To have a woman in a powerful position, equal to that of a male who is also in a powerful position, can send a good message. It's something that they should know. (T[94])

His female partner said that most male offenders begin to appreciate having a woman involved in therapy when they are taking part in a confrontational group:

> Many of these men respond to the nurturing part of me. I don't go in and attack them. I make it quite clear right up front why I am there, and that I don't like what they have done, and that people have been hurt. (T[85])

She agreed with her male cotherapist that they would not accommodate the wish of a client to be seen only by a male.

That just is indicative of some of the person's problems. I have worked with groups where there are some men who have some very serious issues around women, which is part of their problem. Take a rapist: power and control. Here is a female who has got some authority, and that's part of what this fellow needs. We found that sometimes I, as a woman, will pick up on things that my male counterpart won't. (T[85])

Not all therapist pairs have a male and female therapist. Some team leaders were men, and other therapists said that under some conditions it would be all right for a male therapist to see a male offender individually. Nevertheless, for those who believe strongly that attitudes toward women must change, there is little room for negotiation about the sex of therapist.

Alcohol and Drug Abuse

Especially at the beginning of treatment, therapists and clients often see (or describe) the offense differently in terms of the role of alcohol and drug abuse. Both clients we interviewed were told in treatment groups that drugs and alcohol were just an excuse, a way of avoiding responsibility for the offense. But both used the excuse, anyway. Here is Morgan's comment:

I thought it was out of character for me; but I guess anyone can end up in that situation—I started drinking, being lonesome, marital problems, financial problems. There is so much, you know. (C[91])

Jake not only blamed drinking but disputed the argument that it is not an acceptable reason for offending. He claimed that he had been turning his life around by controlling his drinking at the moment he was charged for abusing his youngest granddaughter.

So I had started my own healing, especially the drinking problem. I had started on that two or three years before. Now, like everybody else, I had run into problems. You don't always be successful right off at the start. It takes a few tries at it, and I know it is no excuse for—they don't accept drinking as an excuse for those things. But if people have blackouts—which I did, a lot of other people do—there are times when you are drinking that you do things that you don't remember or probably wouldn't do if you weren't drinking. So drinking has a lot to do with it, let's face it. (C[92])

Therapists will not tolerate that excuse. Here is the view of the psychologist who had written a book on relapse prevention:

> People say, "I did it because I was drunk. I wouldn't have done it if I wasn't drinking that night." What we usually find with those participants is they actually planned doing offenses. Their behavior is starting to steer towards actually acting out their fantasies, and the opportunity simply presented itself. If it hadn't been that they were drinking that night and they saw a woman by her car in a darkened parking lot, it would have been three weeks later picking up a female hitchhiker in the rain. They were pretty close to the point of actually going through with the offense anyway. (T[94])

There is little to say about this disagreement between clients and therapists, and it is probably not realistic to consider it as a matter for negotiation. Offenders often use drugs and alcohol as an excuse, and therapists do not accept it.

Victims Who Abuse

A more serious disagreement between therapist and client, and among therapists, has to do with sex offenders who were once victims themselves. The disagreement focuses on two issues: How common is it for offenders to have been victims, and what difference does it make? Is offending in some sense "caused" by having been abused? If so, should early victimization be a focus of treatment? While some clients and therapists say yes, some therapists believe that offenders merely use their own victimization, whether real or not, as one more excuse.

Both points of view are represented in the literature. Hilton says the rate of victimization among sex offenders, while it may be higher than that for the general population, is no higher than for persons accused of other sorts of crimes. She says there is no reason for therapists to believe that victimization contributes to child molesting "or that empathy can be used to break the victim-offender link." She adds, however, that "Child molesters find this reason appealing" (1993, p. 291).

On the other hand, Orr (1991) maintains that we should take seriously the possibility that childhood sexual abuse, which she believes is common in the background of adult and adolescent offenders, may have causal implications. If so, therapists should consider victimization in planning treatment. She says that a psychodynamic approach would look at the trauma caused by early victimization—speculating that the closer the relationship, the greater the trauma. From a social learning perspective, if the person who abused the offender is seen to be attractive, prestigious, competent, and powerful, there is more likelihood that the offender will see his own abuser as a model and will imitate the abusive behavior.

Whether or not there is evidence of victimization, some therapists see victimization as an excuse that is often used by offenders. We interviewed a child psychiatrist who had testified in several court cases on the issue of whether being abused "causes" later offenses. This was his view:

> People will tell you, "This sex offender was abused in childhood, and now he's abusing. Therefore A caused B." I think that's a mistake. The majority of victims, of course, don't become abusers. What you will hear from people who specialize in working with sex offenders is, "Of course, if you go and ask a sex offender whether he has been abused, he will say that he has because it gets him off the hook." It's easy to say, "I'm a poor victim, therefore I abuse." The two worst adolescent sex offenders that I've seen gave no convincing history of being sexual abused. (T[40])

A female occupational therapist told us that, while some offenders use being victimized as an excuse, for others it is a serious matter. She was a survivor of abuse herself, and her professional practice was with other survivors. But she volunteered to work with an offenders' group to gain insight into their motivation, and co-led the group for a year.

> Some of the men I was very empathic towards. They had been really badly abused themselves. I think a few of them were genuinely sorry—felt really bad and were able to benefit from the help genuinely. I think they all [talked about being abused], but some of them were using that as a rationalization, as an excuse rather than an explanation. (T[57])

In the view of many therapists, the question of victimization is not relevant. The social worker member of our male-female cotherapist pair put it this way:

> We have to be very direct with them. We have to say, "You are here in a sex offender treatment program for your sex offending behavior. Yes, we know you have been victimized, but that is an issue that you are going to have to

deal with separate and apart from what you are here for. For the purpose of this group, the focus is on your offending behavior." (T⁸⁵)

The same point was made by a psychologist who had spent many years working in institutions with adult and youthful offenders:

> We took the position with our group that, if in fact you had been abused, that certainly was a traumatic experience in your life and something that would have to be dealt with. But we were not going to accept that it was the reason for offending or reoffending. If they came to us and said, "I couldn't help it because I have been sexually abused as a child," we would turn to the other 50 percent in the group who hadn't been, and we would say to them, "So what is your excuse then?"
>
> The offenders who have never been victims would point out to them that just wasn't going to slice because it didn't apply in their situation. (T⁵⁵)

This therapist said that offenders grab explanations that they pick up in the popular media.

> One of the big problems is the exposure to things like Oprah and other talk-show hosts who are presenting an awful lot of this material in a very provocative manner. A lot of people are picking up some of these ideas. But they are not sophisticated enough to really know what they are talking about. So they get some of these phrases, "I was abused, so that is why I committed the offense."
>
> The bottom line is, most of them can't tell you why they think it took place other than maybe they got horny and they wanted to have sex. If these guys go to parties and they see that couples are pairing off, they feel that somehow that gives them a right. They think, "Well, I know that so-and-so is going to go to bed with that girl, so I can go to bed with the one that I am with." And they tend to project onto the victims the idea that "Well, if you didn't expect that that was going to happen to you, what the hell are you doing here at this kind of a party?" (T⁵⁵)

There is clearly a line that most therapists take with offenders that minimizes victimization of the offender as an underlying factor. Therapists freely share this with the offender and use other group members to stop the offender from talking about victimization—at least as a cause of their behavior.

There are contexts in which some therapists do find it appropriate to deal with the abuse history of abusers. One such context is in work with adolescents who have been offenders and victims in the same time period. I have introduced a social worker who specializes in therapy with such adolescents. This therapist talked about the etiological interaction between victimization and offending in children:

> My work involves, primarily, children who were victimized sexually by a number of perpetrators and are now committing sexual offenses themselves. And these weren't the children who were just playing doctor. These were the children who were actively going out and coercing or bribing and seducing other child victims. The age range, when I first became involved, was anywhere from twelve to sixteen. Now we are finding that we are getting them as young as nine and ten, and certainly the adolescents who I am working with now experienced their first sexual assault at the age of five and began sexually abusing other children, themselves, about the age of eight or nine.
>
> These kids have sort of a dual identity of both victim and offender. Coming into the program, many of them are still being offended against, and they experience safety for the first time when they come into one of our facilities. Also, their sexual activity with other children is curtailed at the same time.
>
> All of my population experience poor impulse control. and, interestingly enough, all of them want to stop sexually offending to the point where the majority of my adolescent boys have used drugs and alcohol as a means to suppress the urge to sexually offend. (T[79])

It is interesting to contrast this view of the adolescent offender as taking drugs or alcohol to *dampen* the urge to commit an offense, when so many adult sex offenders use substance abuse as an excuse for offending.

She pointed out that this treatment population presents its own unique set of problems. Consider, for instance, the therapist who is dealing with a boy as the victim of abuse, without knowing that the boy is also a perpetrator:

> Often they go in and talk about their sexual abuse and the therapist is extremely supportive and empathic but, in the process, communicates to the boy what an injustice was done by the offender. And here they are holding this secret that they are also an offender. So then what they do? Being black-and-white thinkers, they say, "Well, this person will really think that I am an

asshole and I should be locked away and I am a real bad person." And they go away with that message. (T[79])

The link between being abused and abusing may be more likely to be considered a valid treatment topic when working with adolescents, especially when the client is offender and victim at virtually the same time. Even in dealing with adult offenders, however, not all therapists ignore the offender's own claims of being abused. I have argued that treatment options are related to an underlying conception of the problem. Nowhere is that more true than in the different approaches taken in treatment of sex offenders depending on what the therapist takes to be the cause of offending.

We interviewed a therapist who works exclusively with offenders in prison. He began his work while a Christian minister doing counseling. His work became known and respected, and soon the prison system was deliberately routing sex offenders to his prison so that he could work with them.

He decided to return to school and got two degrees in psychology. He continued his work in prison while pursuing his advanced training and did his thesis research with jailed sex offenders. His strongest research finding was that the offenders were extremely high on measures of dissociation. And the more violent the offenses had been, and the higher the number of victims involved, the more dissociation he found. This led him to take a treatment approach with dissociation as its focus, based on the controversial assumption that most (perhaps all) sex offenders have been sexually abused and feel compelled to abuse others in the same way.

> There's a real sense of trance around this, almost a blacking out. Sometimes you'll see with somebody who has a lot of victims, that there's a ritual around the victimization and that ritual [relates to] what happened to them. It's really an re-enactment.
>
> I started working from a dissociative perspective [using] almost hypnotherapy. What we're trying to is connect them up to themselves. They've sort of put a wall around their own abuse.
>
> A lot of people will say, "Well, how come somebody who's been abused and would know what it was like can go and do that to another person?" But there's a numbness there to what's really happening. So what we try

to do is use techniques that connect them to themselves—their own abuse. If that is successful, that's the best form of empathy training that you can do. All of a sudden he's now feeling his own pain and responding—maybe to something he felt as a kid. It's been blocked out but now he's beginning to feel and experience it. If that happens, he begins to appreciate what's happened, and there's a genuine depth of remorse that starts to emerge at that point. (T[43])

Most group programs we encountered insist that offenders openly admit their offenses. This therapist took a different view. He felt that such admissions did not mean much. He focused on helping offenders feel the pain of their *own* abuse, linking it to the pain their victims must have felt.

One thing you'll hear about perpetrators is that there's a lot of denial and there is a lot projection of blame onto the victims—and that's true. And you can browbeat them into saying, "Okay, yeah, I should have known better. I shouldn't have done it." But if at an emotional level they are able to begin to appreciate it, the owning of responsibility is much deeper. (T[43])

This therapist works with the offender's history of victimization. What about those offenders who were never abused? We asked if he screened out offenders who had no apparent history of abuse. He said no, because he believed they all did, even if they could not remember it. He told us that 60 per cent say they have been abused and 40 per cent say they were not, but "my hypothesis would be that they all are."

This therapist clearly had compassion for his clients, many of whom were violent and had abused many victims. He came by his empathy in a way that might seem paradoxical:

When I was a young fellow I was abused, and I think synchronicity or something got me here and got me involved. I think that part of the reason was just my own victimization and being able to work with that over the years, and I guess healing myself. I think that the seeds are in all of us to be perpetrators—for those of us who have been victims, maybe more so. I guess I could have been a perpetrator as well, so I realized somewhere along the line, I could have been sitting on the other side of the fence. That is a helpful realization. (T[43])

We heard therapists make harsh comments about sex offenders. In the view of this therapist, many mental health professionals who work with offenders are too punitive.

> If you don't work through your biases, they get projected onto your clients. You tend to become abusive to the people you work with, or you tend to treat them as objects, you know: "We are going to fix you."
>
> Some of my experience with people who have been through this kind of "being fixed" thing is they end up with more shame or being more exposed at the end than when they went in, [because professionals] haven't developed the empathy or the ability to respond to the issue in depth. They're pushing at it: "You've got to get the stuff out." But they can't deal with it when it comes out. My experience of talking with guys who have been through that is—"I feel like I have been dissected and my stuff is out there lying all over the place and they have just walked away."
>
> I've been to enough conferences to hear sex offenders bashed by treatment providers. It's abusive. What [offenders] have done is not very likable, but they're victims the same as anybody else. (T[43])

Summary

As we have seen, there is little negotiation in therapy with sex offenders. To some extent, this is a function of the place of treatment in the legal system. Some offenders are in prison when they are treated; others are on probation. But therapists generally welcome the legal framework and use it to motivate their clients to attend and to stay in therapy.

Although there are some treatment options, these are generally not discussed with clients. Choice of therapy depends solely on the therapist's beliefs about the problem and about what works to alleviate it.

This is surprising, since offenders can differ in ways that have been shown to affect treatment and rate of reoffending. There are male and female offenders. Among the males, who are more prevalent, there are offenders who abuse boys and those who abuse girls. Furthermore, some offenders are predators who seek out comparative strangers, while others are incest abusers who may have one or a few victims within the family. Offenders can be divided into those who have and those who have not been abused themselves (which may affect the potential for empathy with the victim). Among incest offenders, some are fixated, and some are regressed.

Finally, among the regressed offenders, some are passive-dependent, while others are aggressive-dominant.

At the very least, this variation among sexual offenders casts doubt on using a single approach for all. The current popularity of packaged group programs probably shortchanges differences among offenders that need to be addressed for optimal outcome.

7

■ ■   ■   ■   ■   ■   ■   ■   ■

Conclusion

Therapy as Negotiated Transition

WE ARE CAUGHT in the middle of our lives trying to anchor the present in a dimly perceived past and an uncertain future. In Emerson's words, "We wake and find ourselves on a stair; there are stairs below us, which we seem to have ascended; there are stairs above us, many a one, which go upward and out of sight" (1969/1844, p. 141).

Our lives, when we reflect, seem to be made up of a series of transitions. Often those moments did not seem so as we lived them and take on that significance only in retrospect. But there are transitions we perceive at the time; graduation, a wedding, the birth of a child all seem to be a transition from one sort of life to another. They fit what Kermode (1967) calls the *myth of transition*. This myth, like the search for origins and the sense of an ending, helps give meaning to our lives. A transition is always from something to something and is an important feature of narrative structure.

Psychotherapy is, for the client, a transition point that is apparent even while it is being lived. One embarks upon therapy with the idea that it will lead to something new. Old problems will be resolved, their causes will be understood and dealt with, and one will be better able to plot the trajectory into the future.

This is asking a lot of therapy, of course, but we often expect more than we get from the transition myth. People marry and divorce, quit jobs and seek new ones, often overestimating what the transition will mean to their lives. But we continue to believe that we can make changes that will bring us brighter prospects. To quote Kermode again, "When we refuse to be dejected by disconfirmed predictions we are asserting a permanent need to live by the pattern rather than the fact" (1967, p. 11).

In this chapter, I approach therapy in its narrative mode—beginning, middle, and end—and see what we can make of it after the voyage through many interviews with therapists and clients. The beginning involves the search for origins of the problem. The middle is therapy itself, the anticipated turning point in one's life. The end is all those notions about what can come out of treatment. In each section I return to the theme of the book and consider what we may have learned about negotiation of consent. Finally, I talk more generally about the therapeutic as well as the ethical value of negotiation.

Beginning: The Search for Origins

In anchoring our narratives, we want to know how things started. People come into therapy not just because they need some current condition alleviated but also because they have a strong need to find out how things got this way. A client told us about her motivation for therapy while she was a bulimic teen-ager: "I used to think, 'Why am I doing this?' And that's when I finally went to the therapist to see if she could figure out why."

The same longing to understand origins was expressed by Morgan, one of the two sex offenders we interviewed. "My biggest problem was I wanted to know. I knew I committed the offense, but I wanted to know why. I racked my brains over it." He felt there had to be some deep-rooted cause to explain what he had done. "You don't just wake up some morning and say, 'Well, I'm going to go commit a sexual assault.'" He had become convinced, listening to members of his treatment group, that sexual offending is often a result of being abused oneself. But he was at a loss to explain his own offense because "I was not a victim, and this is what I couldn't understand."

The need to find origins is sometimes facilitated by therapists and sometimes resisted. Some are schooled in models, including psychoanalysis and some forms of feminist therapy, in which the search for origins is legitimate and important. Others, including gestalt therapists and some cognitive-behavioral therapists, prefer to work with what the client is experiencing now.

Therapy can be undermined if the therapist and the client want to go in different directions. That happened in the case of a young woman who was trying to come to terms with sexual abuse by two babysitters, one of whom later hanged himself. Her cognitive-behavioral therapist was future oriented; the client wanted to understand her past. "Things that I felt were the reason—I don't know whether they *were* the reason or not, but I wanted to deal with some of those issues." She perceived the therapist as saying, "Look to the future, forget the past." The client said, "I just couldn't. . . . That's when I decided to leave her."

In two of the domains we looked at, early trauma was often considered to be the foundation for later problems: in chapter 4, eating disorders; in chapter 6, sex offenses. Therapists were more likely to explore early trauma in the first case than in the second. Therapists tend to believe that even when a sex offender probably was abused as a child, the danger of exploring the past is that the offender will feel encouraged to use the early events as an excuse rather than taking responsibility for current behavior. In the third domain, early childhood sexual abuse, clients often presented post-traumatic problems; the question was whether to look behind these problems and focus on the traumas.

Therapists have different models for determining the usual origin of a given problem. In the best examples, they use their models while acknowledging that every case is different and departs from the model in some way. In other examples, though, therapists indicated to us that they almost always applied their model to a given group. A striking example was the psychoanalytic psychologist who claimed that women with eating disorders never want a female therapist and that he would never make a referral to one. This doctrinaire approach reflected his view of the origin of eating disorders in women: "Remember, they're the 'little girls,' and they're desperately seeking some bond with a father image. They're out to fight the mother." His approach contrasted with that of a cognitive-behavioral therapist who located eating disorders in the daughter-*father* relationship. As one of her clients said, after quitting therapy, "I would have loved to blame it on my father. I didn't like my father very much and if I could make him feel guilty for an eating disorder, then great! But I knew that wasn't the sole reason. And here she was telling me: 'Work things out with your father and I think you'll be all right.'"

Even within problem domains, therapists differ about whether they should engage in a search for origins. A feminist therapist told us that, while many of her colleagues stick with the here and now, she believed that "before someone can change their behavior, they have to understand it." And that understanding, in her view, comes from exploring origins.

The importance of underlying factors as a topic for therapy suggests several areas of negotiation between therapist and client. First, there is the question of whether origins matter at all. Therapists and clients need to come to some workable arrangement in which they do or do not make the client's history a focus of therapy.

If therapist and client decide that at some point they need to focus on origins, they may differ about what those origins are likely to be. Therapists are guided to some extent by their theoretical approaches and by their clinical experience. Clients have their own lived experience as a guide. They can be quite resistant to any perceived invalidation of that experience. As one client told us, "It is my life. It is my body, and I know what is going on in here better than you do. I don't like being a piece of meat and you are trying to figure out what is the matter with the meat." Some therapists put a high value on protecting the validity of the patient's experience. As a therapist remarked, "I don't see *me* as the expert on *their* experience. I see me as a person who has particular skills that I can bring to them. But they have the expertise on themselves."

It may be a problem if the client is resistant to the therapist's model. But our interviews with clients (and, to some extent, with therapists) suggest that a greater danger is the therapist who applies a theory without taking sufficient account of the client's lived experience as the client remembers and understands it. To quote Emerson again, "I have learned that I cannot dispose of other people's facts; but I possess such a key to my own as persuades me . . . that they also have a key to theirs" (1969/1844, p. 159).

Therapists may well need to discuss their own models of how problems start, just as they expect clients to offer opinions about how the problem seemed to start in their own lives. If therapists share their views about typical origins, the client can judge, and reflect on, how the model fits his or her personal experience.

Middle: The Process of Psychotherapy

If therapy is one of those life events that is seen at the time as a moment of transition, how will the transition be accomplished? This is a key question to be negotiated between therapist and client. It begins in the first session, with the formal obtaining of consent (both specific consent and discussion of possible alternatives). It continues throughout treatment as goals are modified, as therapist and client come to understand each other, and as their ideas about origins and endings become more clearly defined.

We have heard from therapists with many different points of view on how much discussion there should be between therapist and client, what the discussion should involve, and when it should happen. We have heard, too, from clients who almost always told us that, when they were dissatisfied, the reason was that there was too little discussion or the therapist wanted to take treatment in a direction that did not match their own experience or suit their goals.

As an extreme example of failure to negotiate, there was the client who recalled visiting a psychiatrist when she was an adolescent with an eating disorder. She and her mother both attended the first (and only) session. "He wouldn't let me talk. I would try and interrupt him, to get that little word in edgewise and contradict him or something, and he would just, 'Nah, nah, nah—just wait; I'll give you a chance to talk at the end.' It was the funniest thing. I just sort of sat there and listened to him preach at me. When we came out we started to laugh about it."

I noted in chapter 1 that there is increasing pressure on health professionals, including psychotherapists, to tell clients about alternatives to the sort of treatment the professional is offering. Some therapists interpret this zeitgeist to mean that they should mention various things they might do but not necessarily talk about forms of treatment they cannot provide or to which they do not subscribe. They fear that the client will be overwhelmed by options, some of which may be unavailable; that client confidence will be undermined; or, in the case of referral, that the client will feel rejected. We found that there is some basis for all of these concerns. Nevertheless, the current legal view is that a health professional should not keep information from clients for any of these reasons (see Rozovsky and Rozovsky, 1990).

Another way of dealing with alternatives, one that some therapists use in the first session, is to describe their own sort of therapy and the reasons for doing it. Then they make it clear that if the client does not like the approach, he or she can go elsewhere. One feminist therapist told clients who were skeptical about feminism that if they did not like it, they "should go somewhere else." Another therapist said that, when clients mention some form of treatment that she does not offer, "I try to refer them to someone who can do that for them. Right away. There is no need to hang on to someone who wants a different type of treatment."

The take-it-or-leave-it approach may fulfill narrowly conceived ethical requirements, but it falls short of the type of negotiation envisioned in this book. Clients who are told in the first session that they can go elsewhere are not being given a choice; they are just being abandoned. The lack of discussion about ways to think about the problem also short-circuits a genuine therapeutic partnership.

Another strategy used by some therapists is to go as far as they can with their own approach. If it does not seem to be working, or if the patient is dissatisfied, then they will talk about referral to someone else for another sort of treatment. As a psychologist explained, "I would tell them about these other things if they became unhappy with their treatment. Or if they were not making progress." This seems less like negotiation than a way of giving up on the client; little wonder that the client might see it as rejection. It always carries the threat that if the client questions the therapist's views—for instance, about the dynamics underlying a particular problem—the client will be cut loose. This is rather like calling divorce threats "negotiation" in marriage.

We heard an excellent analysis from one client of the reason that therapists should discuss alternatives before the therapy starts to break down. "They may not go back, and they may not try and find something else. Because if you haven't let them know that there's something else, they may just think that that's what therapy is."

Many therapists did believe strongly in negotiating with their clients. They engaged in the process not merely because of ethical or legal requirements but because they felt it was an essential component of therapy. A community mental health nurse said that, by offering a variety of possible techniques within the context of a secure therapeutic relationship, the therapist relieves the client of a feeling of failure if some technique fails. "You can suggest something, and, if it doesn't work, we'll try something else. Doesn't mean that they've failed. It just means it may not fit with their personality. It takes off the pressure and enhances the chances of something working."

If our interviews showed extremes in failures to negotiate ("Nah, nah, nah—just wait; I'll give you a chance to talk at the end"), there were also extremes in offering alternatives. In one case, the therapist's procedure included offering alternatives she herself had never heard of. She told young women with eating disorders to go and look in the library and find popular books, autobiographies, and so on. The clients were to come back and tell her what seemed to fit them and what sort of treatment they thought might be helpful. Some clients were, not surprisingly, disenchanted when they brought up cases and treatments the therapist didn't seem to know. "Somebody read one I wasn't familiar with. . . . I remember saying at the time, did she have it with her? Because I'd like to go through it and read it. . . . I think she didn't come back." Although I have offered reasons why therapists should offer alternatives, there is no need to go quite *that* far.

Another approach that seems egalitarian (though it may not be, and it may have other drawbacks) was that of a therapist who handed the *Diagnostic and Statistical Manual* to clients and let them read through lists of symptoms and decide what diagnosis fit their case. "The very documents I use to come to a diagnosis I put in their hands and say, 'Look, this is what I'm thinking about. Have a look at these symptoms. According to this, if you have six out of these nine symptoms, then you probably have this disorder. Let's go through them and see. What do you think?'" This seems to be a way to convince clients that they do have the problem the therapist says they have, rather than a genuine negotiating strategy.

There was a further reason for therapists' reluctance to discuss their goals for therapy: The therapist might want the client to change in ways to which the client would object. One controversial current theory about treatment suggests that therapists should be paternalistic if they think they know what is best for the client, even if the client disagrees. This theory has its origins in therapy with battered women. It is often assumed that battered women need to feel autonomy and a sense of agency in their lives; they need to start making their own choices. The problem is that, when offered choices, they sometimes opt to return to the abusive spouse, where, presumably, their independence is severely diminished. This paradox has led some therapists to encourage women to leave their spouses, not as an option but as a goal of treatment.

Huston (1984) spoke for those who take this position. She noted that ethics codes tend to value both autonomy and client welfare. She advocated what she called a weak paternalistic stance: Get the client to agree to leave her spouse, and, when she has some practice making her own decisions again, permit more autonomy in therapy. The theory is that a battered woman has limited competence to make rational judgments: "The person's behavior is substantially nonvoluntary" (p. 830). Presumably this rationale for paternalism could be applied to other problem domains. To take an uncharitable view, the client is seen as irrational as long as he or she does not make the sorts of decisions that the therapist thinks are best; one should not let irrational people make bad choices.

A stronger answer than I could possibly make to this antinegotiation stance was expressed by one of our participants. She was a young psychologist who worked in a rural setting where she saw many traditional families. Their views of the good life were probably very different from her own. Did she have a mandate to change their values, while supposedly working on some other problem they brought to therapy? She had serious doubts about that. "If a family is happy with the way things are, who am I to come in and muck it up? Just because they come to see me, does that mean that they are giving consent for me to fix whatever I think is wrong? I don't think so."

We are now moving into the question of what therapists should or should not try to change in the client. That leads us to the perceived end toward which the therapy narrative is projected.

Sense of an Ending: Expectations about Outcomes

As a transition episode, the therapy narrative always has some sense of an ending. Transition to what? The client has expectations based on cultural information about therapy, perhaps on previous therapy experience, and particularly on the client's own view of the intractability of the problem. Sometimes the "problem," in fact, seems inseparable from the person. As someone with an eating disorder told us, "I know I'll never be better. This is me. That's the way I am. I'll never ever stop, never. Because it's been going on for so long. It's engraved into my life now. It's a part of me. My doctor said, 'Why are you doing this?' And I said 'Because I don't want to die fat.'"

This pessimism is a common theme for clients and former clients in the domain of eating disorders. Even among those who had stopped engaging in anorexic or bulimic behaviors, the obsession with food lived on. A young woman who had experienced a frightening anorexic episode when she was a teen-ager told us: "I don't think I'll ever be unneurotic about food." Although she was free of symptoms and expected to remain so, she said she was still obsessed with weight. "I really don't bother dieting, but I always think I should be."

Sexual abuse survivors also tend to suffer long-term consequences for which therapy offers no quick fix. They have great difficulty learning to trust when their childhood trust has been so betrayed. A good therapeutic alliance might help them trust their therapist; that trust might spread to some other people. But they probably never lose the sense of living in a profoundly unsafe world.

We interviewed only two clients who were sex offenders, but each seemed to represent a particular type described in the literature and by therapists. One was a multiple incest offender whose optimism about healing himself was patently defensive. The other had molested a young boy outside his family. In theory he was at a much higher risk to reoffend. But the shame he felt, and his terror of going back to jail, provided the motivation that might make for success in his recidivism prevention program.

In both cases, whatever the behavioral outcomes, there was no suggestion that there would be much change in the fact that children would continue to be a source of arousal. Again, there was no "cure" on the horizon. Two treatments that are supposed to dampen sexual arousal, medication for hormone control and castration, are not popular in North America. Even if they work, they reduce arousal without changing the object of desire. Aversive conditioning, a treatment intended to rechannel sexual feelings, has been socially stigmatized.

Some clients direct their interest in their own problem into an effort to become therapists themselves. One former client who had had an eating disorder became a dietitian partly as a way of dealing with her constant interest in food. We heard about prisoners who become enthusiastic facilitators in group programs for sex offenders. Many survivors of sexual abuse try to help others. Sometimes, like JV, they work with other abuse victims. Sometimes they volunteer to visit groups of sex offenders in empathy-training attempts.

Health professionals, too, need a sense of an ending to the therapy narrative. And they often have to come to terms with results that are helpful but fall short of a real "cure." Physicians who are accustomed to this situation when dealing with physical complaints may lose perspective when the problem is psychological and thus, they think, under the client's control. A client told us about the rage of her physician: "He got mad—swore at me—threatened me." She had another physician who had the opposite reaction: "In passing, he'd say, 'So how's the eating disorder going? . . . Still doing it?'" This sort of professional nonchalance is, of course, a defense against feeling helpless and hopeless.

Psychotherapists need to believe in the possibility of positive outcomes to make their enterprise worthwhile. One therapist talked about the frustration of doing the best you can but not seeing positive change in clients. "We really do want our clients to get better," she said. "We feel like were doing everything we've been trained to do, and it isn't working. And so, instead of saying, 'Maybe what I need to do is rethink how I'm doing this, or try to discover new ways of handling this, or refer to people who may have better luck,' what we do is get mad at the patient, say, well, they're hopeless and useless."

We found that therapists have various coping strategies. One psychologist emphasized "hope" with his clients, even though he, himself, was profoundly pessimistic. He said he told them over and over, "I think you can do it; you can try." But he told us that clients' basic dynamics never change.

A psychiatrist also thought that his own therapy was of little use for eating disorders, but he could project a happy end, anyway. He advocated love, marriage, and children: "In all of the cases I have dealt with in great depth, none of them were fully cured until they were married and had a child; that seems to stabilize everything." A psychologist who took a similar view tried to promote such attachment in his therapy with survivors of sexual abuse. One of his clients told us, "For two or three years he focused on how to get me involved with a man—suggesting personal ads, 'you could hire a match maker. . . . We've got to get you a man.'"

Most therapists we interviewed seemed to have made peace with the intractable nature of psychological problems. They believed there is value in having clients stop life-threatening starvation, whether or not they ever become "unneurotic about food." There is value in having survivors of sexual abuse learn to trust some people even if they never lose a general sense of betrayal. And there is value in having sex offenders curb their dangerous behavior, whatever the direction of their latent desires.

Complex Problems and Simple Solutions

If I were to sum up in one sentence the lesson about psychotherapy to be learned from this study, it would be this: The best therapy takes account of the complexities of the client's lived experience; the worst therapy imposes a simple structure into which that experience must fit.

If that observation is true, what accounts for the simplifying of complex problems? There seem to be two sources of simplistic solutions. One is the therapist's training and orientation, including the therapist's understanding of current research, which provide a model for understanding a given psychological problem. The second is the therapist's experience with many clients who have the same diagnosis—experience that can create simple stereotypes.

Donald Polkinghorne (1991, 1996) has argued that therapists build up a knowledge base in their practices that is independent of any body of research about psychological problems and their treatment. We found that many therapists relied upon this clinical lore, rather than on reference to controlled studies. A forensic psychiatrist translated his experience with sex offenders into the bold formulation that when offenders talk about their own abuse, it is always an excuse. A psychologist who worked with sex offenders in prison was just as certain that they had all been abused, even if they denied it or did not remember it. Both relied on what they had seen, rather than on the research literature (which supports neither of these extreme positions).

Although Polkinghorne suggests that clinical knowledge may be a better guide to good therapy than formal research, we found many therapists who relied on their ideas about current research to explain why they did what they did. Virtually all therapists who talked to us about false memory syndrome, for example, made some reference to research. Sometimes they stretched to literature that was only indirectly related, such as the therapist who connected his views about false memories to "all the research that has been done on victim identification."

Formal training provides models that guide practice. But these models can also constrict the therapist's approach to a problem. We interviewed therapists who professed a variety of orientations. Such models are positive when they provide a bedrock of competence in dealing with problems; they are negative when they lead therapists to ignore features that make a particular case different from the model's norms.

There is a dangerous simplicity in relying too much on either clinical experience or on formal models. Two sorts of biases have been identified: availability and representativeness. We know these biases distort judgment in decision making (Kahneman and Tversky, 1972; Tversky and Kahneman, 1973) and in applied psychology (O'Neill, 1981; O'Neill and Trickett, 1982).

Both biases lead therapists to oversimplify the case about which some judgment is being made. The representativeness bias occurs when a theoretical model is imposed on new cases (they are treated as "representative" of the model). The availability bias imposes a stereotype based on cases one has seen previously (and hence salient or "available" to memory). The problem comes not from the model or the experience but from the simplification that neglects unique features of every case. As the saying goes, for every complex problem there is a simple solution, and it is always wrong.

Some therapists are aware of these potential biases and work hard to keep them in check. A psychologist told us that in her training she had never seen a female substance abuser who had not also been sexually abused. She had developed explanations for this apparent link based on the learning theory model to which she subscribed. Thus, she was potentially vulnerable to both sorts of bias, that flowing from theory and that arising from experience. Nevertheless, she was keenly aware of the problem that can occur when "somebody comes in and she's a substance-abusing female, and every other patient you've ever seen that's been a substance abuser also has a history of sexual abuse and physical abuse or some kind of traumatic event." She said it was important to stay tuned to details of each case, despite the lessons of one's training and experience. "I think that you just keep your ears and your eyes open. . . . It is a dangerous thing to make assumptions that the reason this person is substance abusing is because they have had this previous traumatic event, and, if they don't think they have, I'm going to convince them in therapy."

The Therapeutic Value of Negotiating

Discussion between therapist and client is not only an ethical issue; it also has therapeutic value. Therapists in some domains told us about the benefit of negotiation in terms of specific treatment objectives. Therapists dealing with survivors of sexual abuse were likely to see active negotiation as a way of giving control of the process to a client whose history was marked by traumatic loss of control. Opinions were mixed on the value of negotiation when working with anorexic and bulimic patients. Those who saw these illnesses as battles for control worried that negotiating about anything would play into that battle. Those who work with sex offenders had a general bias against negotiation; most saw these clients as manipulative and believed that offering options or discussing causes simply increases the possibilities for manipulation.

Beyond the specifics of these domains, however, I argue that negotiation has a general therapeutic benefit. Therapists have an opportunity to clear up the clients' misconceptions, such as misinformation about nutrition, about who is to blame for childhood sexual abuse, or a pedophile's belief that the abused child has benefited from being "taught" by an adult. Clients may also have misconceptions about therapy and what they can expect from it; these, too, can be clarified in discussion.

While most therapists recognize that negotiation can clear up clients' misconceptions, fewer recognize that negotiation is also a vehicle for clearing up the *therapist's* misconceptions. An open dialogue can make the therapist aware of features of the case that depart from both the therapist's model and his or her previous experience, and thus it serves as a corrective to the representativeness and availability biases.

Finally, negotiation brings together the two different therapy narratives of therapist and client. These two stories, with their beginnings, middles, and ends, must be coordinated for the development of a productive therapeutic experience.

References

American Medical Association. (1847). Code of medical ethics. *Proceedings of the national convention 1846–1847.* pp. 83–106.

American Psychiatric Association. (1989). *The principles of medical ethics with annotations especially applicable to psychiatry.* Washington, D.C.: Author.

American Psychological Association (1990). Ethical principles of psychologists. *American Psychologist, 45,* 390–395.

Anderson, L., and Gold, K. (1994). "I know what it means but it's not how I feel": The construction of survivor identity in feminist counseling practice. *Women & Therapy, 15,* 5–17.

Angus, L., and Hardtke, K. (1994). Narrative processes in psychotherapy. *Canadian Psychology, 35,* 190–203.

Appelbaum, P. S., Lidz, C. W., and Meisel, A. (1987). *Informed consent: Legal theory and clinical practice.* New York: Oxford University Press.

Bakhtin, M. M. (1981). *The dialogic imagination.* Edited by M. Holquist. Austin: University of Texas Press.

Beck, A. T. (1991). Cognitive therapy. *American Psychologist, 46,* 368–375.

Becker, H. (1992). Cases, causes, conjectures, stories, and imagery. In H. Becker and C. Ragin (Eds.), *What is a case?* (pp. 173–202). New York: Cambridge University Press.

Bruner, J. (1990). *Acts of meaning.* Cambridge, Mass.: Harvard University Press.

Canadian Psychological Association. (1988). *Statement on the treatment of sex offenders.* Unpublished report, Ottawa, Canada.

———. (1991). *Canadian code of ethics for psychologists.* Ottawa, Canada: Author.

Canterbury v. Spence. (1972). 464 F2d 772 (District of Columbia Circuit Court).

Charmaz, K. (1983). The grounded theory method: An explication and interpretation. In R. M. Emerson (Ed.), *Contemporary field research* (127–148). Boston: Little, Brown.

———. (1994). Identity dilemmas of chronically ill men. *Sociological Quarterly, 35,* 269–288.

Claude-Pierre, P. (1997). *The secret language of eating disorders: The revolutionary new approach to curing anorexia and bulimia.* Toronto: Random House.

Cobbs v. Grant. (1972). 502 P2d l (California).

Collins, J. (1927). Should doctors tell the truth? *Harper's Monthly Magazine, 155,* p. 320–326.

Eco, U. (1984). *The role of the reader.* Bloomington: Indiana University Press.

Emerson, R. W. (1969/1844). Experience. In R. L. Cook (Ed.), *Ralph Waldo Emerson: Selected prose and poetry.* San Francisco: Rinehart Press.

Evans, D. R. (1997). *The law, standards of practice, and ethics in the practice of psychology.* Toronto, Ontario: Emond Montgomery Publications.

Everstine, L., Everstine, D., Haymann, G., True, R., Frey, D., Johnson, H., and Seiden, R. (1980). Privacy and confidentiality in psychotherapy. *American Psychologist, 35,* 828–840.

Fairburn, C. G. (1997). Interpersonal psychotherapy for bulimia nervosa. In D. M. Garner and P. E. Garfinkel, *Handbook of treatment for eating disorders.* 2d Ed. (pp. 278–294). New York: Guilford Press.

Fine, M. (1994). Working the hyphens: Reinventing self and other in qualitative research. In N. K. Denzin and Y. S. Lincoln (Eds.), *Handbook of qualitative research.* London: Sage.

———. (1996). Writing the wrongs of fieldwork. Paper presented at the Twenty-Sixth International Congress of Psychology, Montreal, August.

Freyd, J. J. (1994). Betrayal trauma: Traumatic amnesia as an adaptive response to childhood abuse. *Ethics & Behavior, 4,* 307–329.

———. (1996). *Betrayal trauma: The logic of forgetting childhood abuse.* Cambridge, Mass.: Harvard University Press.

Garbarino, J. (1997). *Making sense of senseless youth violence.* Paper presented at the Annual Convention of the American Psychological Association, August.

Garner, D. M., and Garfinkel, P. E. (1997). *Handbook of treatment for eating disorders.* 2d Ed. New York: Guilford Press.

Geertz, C. (1973). Thick description: Toward an interpretive theory of culture. In C. Geertz, *The interpretation of cultures* (pp. 3–30). New York: Basic Books.

———. (1983). *Local knowledge.* New York: Basic Books.

Gergen, K. J. (1994). *Realities and relationships.* Cambridge, Mass.: Harvard University Press.

———. (1997). *Constructionist therapy in cultural context.* Paper presented at the Annual Convention of the American Psychological Association, August.

Gergen, K. J., and Kaye, J. (1992). Beyond narrative in the negotiation of therapeutic meaning. In S. McNamee and K. J. Gergen (Eds.), *Therapy as social construction*. London: Sage.

Gergen, M. (1994). Free will and psychotherapy: Complaints of the draughtsmen's daughters. *Journal of Theoretical and Philosophical Psychology, 14,* 13–24.

Giaretto, H., Giaretto, A., and Sgroi, S. M. (1978). Co-ordinated community treatment of incest. In A. W. Burgess, A. N. Groth, L. L. Holmstrom, and S. M. Sgroi (Eds.), *Sexual assault of children and adolescents*. Lexington, Mass.: Lexington Books.

Gillies, L. A., Hashmall, J. M., Hilton, N. Z., and Webster, C. D. (1992). Relapse prevention in pedophiles: Clinical issues and program development. *Canadian Psychology, 33,* 199–208.

Gilligan, C. (1982). *In a different voice: Psychological theory and women's development*. Cambridge, Mass.: Harvard University Press.

———. (1991). *The psyche lives in a medium of culture: How then shall we speak of love?* Annual Convention of the American Psychological Association, San Francisco, August.

Goldner, E. M., Birmingham, C. L., and Smye, V. (1997) Addressing treatment refusal in Anorexia Nervosa: Clinical, ethical, and legal considerations. In D. M. Garner and P. E. Garfinkel (Eds.), *Handbook of treatment for eating disorders*. 2d Ed. (pp. 450–461). New York: Guilford Press.

Grice, P. (1989). *Studies in the way of words*. Cambridge, Mass.: Harvard University Press.

Groth, A. N., and Birnbaum, H. J. (1978). Adult sexual orientation and the attraction to underage persons. *Archives of Sexual Behavior, 7,* pp. 197–181.

Guba, E. G., and Lincoln, Y. S. (1994). Competing paradigms in qualitative research. In N. K. Denzin and Y. S. Lincoln (Eds.), *Handbook of qualitative research* (pp. 105–117). Thousand Oaks, Calif.: Sage.

Hacking, I. (1991). Two souls in one body. *Critical Inquiry, 17,* 838–867.

———. (1995). *Rewriting the soul: Multiple personality and the sciences of memory*. Princeton, N.J.: Princeton University Press.

Hare-Mustin, R. T., Marecek, J., Kaplan, A. G., and Liss-Levinson, N. (1995). Rights of clients, responsibilities of therapists. In D. N. Bersoff (Ed.), *Ethical conflicts in psychology* (pp. 305–310). Washington, D.C.: American Psychological Association.

Highlen, P. S., and Hill, C. E. (1984). Factors affecting client change in individual counseling: Current status and theoretical speculations. In S. D. Brown and R. W. Lent (Eds.), *Handbook of counseling psychology* (pp. 334–396). New York: Wiley.

Hilton, N. Z. (1993). Childhood sexual victimization and lack of empathy in child molesters: Explanation or excuse? *International journal of offender therapy and comparative criminology, 37,* 287–296.

Hippocrates (1923/c. 400 B.C.). Oath; Precepts; Decorum. *Loeb Classical Library*. Cambridge, Mass.: Harvard University Press.

Hooker, W. (1849). *Physician and patient.* New York: Baker and Scribner.

Howard, G. S. (1991). Culture tales: A narrative approach to thinking, cross-cultural psychology, and psychotherapy. *American Psychologist, 46,* 187–197.

Hunt v. Bradshaw. (1955). 242 N.C. 517, 88 SE2d, 766.

Huston, K. (1984). Ethical decisions in treating battered women. *Professional Psychology: Research and Practice, 15,* 822–832.

Kahneman, D., and Tversky, A. (1972). Subjective probability: A judgment of representativeness. *Cognitive Psychology, 3,* 430–454.

Kermode, F. (1967). *The sense of an ending.* Oxford: Oxford University Press.

Kidder, L. H. (1981). Qualitative research and quasi-experimental frameworks. In M. B. Brewer and B. E. Collins (Eds.), *Scientific inquiry and the social sciences.* San Francisco: Jossey-Bass.

———. (1982). Face validity from multiple perspectives. In D. Brinberg and L. H. Kidder (Eds.), *New directions for methodology of social and behavioral science: Forms of validity in research* (No. 12, pp. 41–57). San Francisco: Jossey-Bass.

Kidder, L. H., and Fine, M. (1987). Qualitative and quantitative methods: When stories converge. In M. M. Mark and R. L. Shotland (Eds.), *Multiple methods in program evaluation* (pp. 57–75). San Francisco: Jossey-Bass.

———. (1997). Qualitative inquiry in psychology: A radical tradition. in D. Fox and I. Prilleltensky (Eds.), *Critical psychology: An introduction.* London: Sage Publications.

King, S. W. (1975). *Communication and social influence.* Reading, Mass.: Addison-Wesley.

Kirschner, S. R. (1997). *Are critiques of constructionism valid?* Paper presented at the Annual Convention of the American Psychological Association, Chicago, August.

Knapp, S. J., and Vandecreek, L. (1997). *Treating patients with memories of abuse: Legal risk management.* Washington, D.C.: American Psychological Association.

Kvale, S. (1992). Postmodern psychology: A contradiction in terms? In S. Kvale (Ed.), *Psychology and postmodernism.* London: Sage.

Laidlaw, T. A. (1990). Dispelling the myths: A workshop on compulsive eating and body image. In T. A. Laidlaw, C. Malmo, and Associates (Eds.), *Healing voices: Feminist approaches to therapy with women* (pp. 15–32). San Francisco, Calif.: Jossey-Bass.

Laidlaw, T. A., Malmo, C., and Associates (1990). *Healing voices: Feminist approaches to therapy with women.* San Francisco, Calif.: Jossey-Bass.

Langevin, R., Wright, P., and Handy, L. (1988). What treatment do sex offenders want? *Annals of sex research, 1,* 401–415.

Lazarsfeld, P. F. (1972/1936). The art of asking why. In P. F. Lazarsfeld, *Qualitative analysis: Historical and critical essays* (pp. 183–202). Boston: Allyn and Bacon.

Loftus, E. (1993). The reality of repressed memories. *American Psychologist, 48,* 518–537.

———. (1994). The repressed memory controversy. *American Psychologist, 49,* 443–445.

Loftus, E., and Ketcham, K. (1994). *The myth of repressed memories.* New York: St. Martin's Press.

Lyddon, W. J. (1989). Personal epistemology and preference for counseling. *Journal of Counseling Psychology, 36,* 423–429.

Mahmood, H. (1995). *Therapists' beliefs and practices regarding informed consent.* Unpublished thesis, Wilfred Laurier University, Waterloo, Ontario, Canada.

Malmo, C. (1990). Recovering the past: using hypnosis to heal childhood trauma. In T. A. Laidlaw, C. Malmo, and Associates (Eds.), *Healing voices: Feminist approaches to therapy with women.* San Francisco, Calif..: Jossey-Bass.

Marecek, J., and Kravetz, D. (1998). Power and agency in feminist therapy. In I. B. Seu and M. C. Heenan (Eds.), *Feminism and psychotherapy: Reflections on contemporary theories and practices.* London: Sage.

Marshall, W. L., Laws, D. R., and Barbaree, H. E. (Eds.). (1990). *Handbook of sexual assault: Issues, theories, and treatment of the offender.* New York: Plenum Press.

McInnes, C. (1997). Victoria clinic under investigation. *The Globe and Mail,* Toronto, Ontario. Nov. 20, A-3.

McMullen, L. M. (1989). Use of figurative language in successful and unsuccessful cases of psychotherapy: Three comparisons. *Metaphor and symbolic activity, 4,* 203–225.

McMullen, L. M., and Conway, J. B. (1994). Dominance and nurturance in the figurative expressions of psychotherapy clients. *Psychotherapy Research, 4,* 43–57.

Minuchin, S., Rosman, B., and Baker, L. (1978). *Psychosomatic families: Anorexia nervosa in context.* Cambridge, Mass.: Harvard University Press.

Mishler, E. G. (1986a). *Research interviewing: Context and narrative.* Cambridge, Mass.: Harvard University Press.

———. (1986b). The analysis of interview-narratives. In T. R. Sarbin (Ed.), *Narrative psychology: The storied nature of human conduct* (pp. 233–255). New York: Praeger.

Mitchell v. Robinson. (1960). 334 SW2d 11 (Missouri).

Natanson v. Kline. (1960). 350 P2d 1093 (Kansas).

National Association of Social Workers. (1989). *NASW standards for the practice of clinical social work.* Silver Spring, Md.: National Association of Social Workers.

Nuremberg Code. (1964/1945) *Science, 143:* 553.

O'Neill, P. (1981). Cognitive community psychology. *American Psychologist, 36,* 457–469.

O'Neill, P., and Trickett, E. J. (1982). *Community consultation.* San Francisco: Jossey-Bass.

Orr, B. Y. (1991). Male adolescent sex offenders: A comparison of two treatment approaches. Special Issue: Child sexual abuse. *Journal of Child and Youth Care*, Fall, 87–101.

Packman, W. L., Cabot, M. G., and Bongar, B. (1994). Malpractice arising from negligent psychotherapy: Ethical, legal, and clinical implications of *Osheroff v. Chestnut Lodge*. *Ethics & Behavior, 4*, 175–197.

Paget, M. (1983). Experience and knowledge. *Human Studies, 6*, 67–90.

Percival, T. (1849). *Medical ethics*. 3d Ed. Oxford: John Henry Parker.

Perls, F. S. (1969). *Gestalt therapy verbatim*. Lafayette, Calif.: Real People Press.

Pithers, W. D., Marques, J. K., Gibat, C. C., and Marlatt, G. A. (1983). Relapse prevention with sexual aggressives: A self-control model of treatment and maintenance of change. In J. G. Greer and I. R. Stuart (Eds.), *The sexual aggressor: Current perspective on treatment* (pp. 214–239). New York: Van Nostrand Reinhold.

Plimpton, G. (1997). Capote's long ride. *New Yorker*, Oct. 13, pp. 62–71.

Polivy, J., and Federoff, I. (1997). Group psychotherapy. In D. M. Garner and P. E. Garfinkel. *Handbook of treatment for eating disorders*. 2d Ed. (pp. 462–475). New York: Guilford Press.

Polkinghorne, D. E. (1991). *Positivism and practice*. American Psychological Association Annual Convention, San Francisco, August.

———. (1996). *Postmodern psychotherapy and the return to phenomenological theory*. American Psychological Association Annual Convention, Toronto, August.

Pope, K. S., and Vasquez, M. J. T. (1991). *Ethics in psychotherapy and counseling: A practical guide for psychologists*. San Francisco: Jossey-Bass.

Reibl v. Hughes. (1980). 2 Supreme Court of Canada 880.

Rozovsky, L., and Rozovsky, F. (1990). *The Canadian law of consent to treatment*. Toronto: Butterworths.

Salgo v. Stanford University. (1957). 317 P2d 170 (California Court of Appeal).

Seidman, I. E. (1991). *Interviewing as qualitative research*. New York: Teachers College Press.

Silverman, W. A. (1989). The myth of informed consent: In daily practice and in clinical trials. *Journal of Medical Ethics, 15*, 6–11.

Spence, D. P. (1986). Narrative smoothing and clinical wisdom. In T. R. Sarbin (Ed.), *Narrative psychology: The storied nature of human conduct* (pp. 211–232). New York: Praeger.

Stone, A. A. (1990). Law, science, and psychiatric malpractice: A response to Klerman's indictment of psychoanalytic psychiatry. *American Journal of Psychiatry, 147*, 419–427.

Tannen, D. (1989). *Talking voices: Repetition, dialogue, and imagery in conversational discourse*. Cambridge: Cambridge University Press.

Tanney, M. F., and Birk, J. M. (1976). Women counselors for women clients?: A review of the research. *Counseling Psychologist, 6*, 28–31.

Terkel, S. (1970). *Hard times: An oral history of the Great Depression.* New York: Random House.

———. (1972). *Working.* New York: Pantheon.

———. (1988). *The great divide: Second thoughts on the American dream.* New York: Pantheon.

Toukmanian, S. G., and Rennie, D. L. (1992). *Psychotherapy process research.* London: Sage.

Tversky, A., and Kahneman, D. (1973). Availability: A heuristic for judging frequency and probability. *Cognitive Psychology, 5,* 207–232.

Vanderlinden, J., Norré, J., and Vandereycken, W. (1992). *A practical guide to the treatment of bulimia nervosa.* New York: Bruner/Mazel.

Vaughn, D. (1992). Theory elaboration: The heuristics of case analysis. In H. Becker and C. Ragin (Eds.), *What is a case?* (pp. 173–202). New York: Cambridge University Press.

Way, N. (1998). *Everyday courage: The lives and stories of urban teenagers.* New York: New York University Press.

Webster's third new international dictionary. (1981). Chicago: Encyclopedia Britannica.

Westcott, M. (1988). *The psychology of human freedom: A human science perspective and critique.* New York: Springer-Verlag.

———. (1992). The discursive expression of human freedom. *American Behavioral Scientist, 36,* 73–87.

———. (1994). Freedom and civilization: When more is less. *Canadian Psychology, 35,* 159–166.

Wong, J. (1989). *Regulation of pornography: The experience of film classifiers.* Unpublished Master's thesis, Acadia University, Wolfville, Nova Scotia, Canada.

World Medical Association (1975). *The declaration of Helsinki.* Reprinted in S. J. Reiser, A. J. Dyck, and W. J. Curran (Eds.), *Ethics in medicine: Historical perspectives and contemporary concerns* (pp. 328–329). Cambridge, Mass.: M.I.T. Press, 1977.

Wormith, J. S., and Hansen, R. K. (1992). The treatment of sexual offenders in Canada: An update. *Canadian Psychology, 33,* 180–198.

Index

■ ■　■　■　　■　　■　　　■　　　■　　　■

About the Author

Patrick O'Neill was born in Vancouver, Canada. As a young man he began a career in the theater, as playwright, actor, and director. He turned to journalism and then child care work before settling on psychology.

His undergraduate studies were at the University of Victoria, and he received his doctorate in clinical-community psychology from Yale University. At Yale, he was associated with the psychoeducational clinic. His interest in community research and intervention led to a collaboration with Edison Trickett on the book *Community Consultation*.

In recent years Professor O'Neill's work has centered on ethical decision making. He lives in Nova Scotia, where he is a Professor of Psychology at Acadia University and an Adjunct Professor at Dalhousie University, teaching ethical decision making at both. He has a strong interest in the often-troublesome interplay between professional ethics and academic freedom, and is chairman of the Academic Freedom and Tenure Committee of the Canadian Association of University Teachers. This book combines his interests in ethical issues, narrative approaches in psychology, and qualitative research.